GOOD LONG TERM CARE -

How to Find it, Get it & Pay for it.

AN ELDER LAW ATTORNEY'S PERSPECTIVE

By Carl B. Zacharia Esq.

This publication was created to provide accurate and authoritative information in regard to the subject matter covered. It is sold with the understanding that the publisher and author is not engaged in rendering legal, accounting, or other professional service. If legal advice or other expert assistance is required, the services of a competent professional should be sought. The legal authorities, statutes, regulations, rules, policies and customs vary from state to state. You are urged and advised to seek out competent legal advice to advise you.

Published by:
Senior Care Resources LLC
111 W. McMurray Road
McMurray, PA 15317
(724) 942-6200

ISBN-13: 9780615768038
ISBN-10: 0615768032

For More Information, Visit our Website: www.GoodLTC.com

ABOUT
THE AUTHOR

Carl B. Zacharia is the managing attorney for Zacharia & Brown with offices in McKeesport and Peters Township in western Pennsylvania. Carl is licensed to practice law in both the Commonwealth of Pennsylvania since 1993 as well as the State of Florida since 1994. In addition to all Courts in Pennsylvania and Florida, he is admitted to practice before the U.S. District Court Western District of Pennsylvania, U.S. Court of Appeals 3rd Circuit, the United States Supreme Court, the U.S. Court of Federal Claims and the United States Circuit Court of Appeals for the Federal Circuit. He received his undergraduate degree from Washington and Jefferson College and his law degree from Duquesne University School of Law, where he was a published member of the Duquesne Law Review and where he served as an associate editor. He is an extensive and frequent lecturer on estate planning and elder law topics. Carl also teaches on the subjects of Elder Law and Estate Planning at Community College of Allegheny County as well as Penn State University. Carl is the developer of SNF Finder, a popular app for iPhones and Android devices. Carl is also a developer of several apps designed for estate and elder law attorneys that operate on Apple IPhone, IPad and Android smartphones and tablets. For more information about these, and other apps, visit www.GoodLTC.com.

ACKNOWLEDGEMENTS

I'd like to thank the attorneys and staff at Zacharia & Brown P.C. and Senior Care Resources LLC for their input and contributions to this book. I'd also like to thank my family for their support. Finally, I'd like to thank the members of our law firm, Christine Brown Murphy, Colleen Bratkovich, Thomas McCaffrey, Justin Ellis, Carrie Conby and Ben Urso. This team at Zacharia & Brown has the vision, dedication and commitment to give us the good name we have in the community for looking to help people at one of the most strenuous times of their lives more so than simply looking out for themselves and trying to make a buck. When you really help people, the benefits, personally, spiritually and financially come automatically. Thank you one and all.

Long term care decision making is a difficult and trying time for anyone. These are major crossroads in one's life and the worries for their loved one, as well as the major changes one's individual life is facing, particularly when your spouse is entering into a nursing home and leaving home for the first time in perhaps many years can be devastating. We try our best to be caring, compassionate and understanding lawyers.

Elder law attorneys are a different breed. To be a capable elder law attorney, one has to be caring, compassionate and tough, sometimes all at the same time. I am proud to be a member of that community.

I hope you enjoy this book. If you have a question or would like to reach me, my email is czacharia@pittsburghelderlaw.com.

Carl B. Zacharia, Esq.
November 2015

TABLE OF CONTENTS

PREFACE

WHO NEEDS THIS BOOK

The world of Long Term Care is better defined as complex than it is complicated. The distinction is subtle. *Complicated* denotes something that requires a high level of skill. *Complex* means that something has many parts or components. The world of long term care does not consist of any one element that is difficult to understand. The problem lies in the interrelationship of all of the elements and how they come together. These complexities give rise to a large and substantial number of traps or pitfalls that exist for the uninitiated.

Because of these complexities, I've written this book and provided reference data to help you find the very best care possible for you or your loved one. In my nearly 20 years of practicing elder law, I've found that it is incredibly difficult to communicate all of the aspects of the various laws and their interplay. It is a very dangerous area for anyone to enter into on their own. This book was designed to help the reader better understand what their elder law attorney is trying to communicate to them. When you are looking for an elder law attorney, or you've just finished your first or second appointment with one, this book will be a handy reference to read to better understand what your options are and how the legal framework will apply to your circumstances.

STATISTICS

Current Statistics for Long Term Care provided by the Centers for Medicare and Medicaid Services. As of November 2015 there are:

- Number of nursing homes: 15,657
- Number of beds: 1,663,840
- Occupancy rate: 81.94 percent
- Number of current residents: 1,363,412
- Average length of stay: 27 months

Very long nursing home stays, generally considered to last five years or more account for nearly one in 10 (8.9%) residents between ages 75 and 84. For those who are 85 years or older, the percentage is higher, closer to 13.2 percent. If you live a long life, the chances of needing long term care which can take place at home or in a skilled facility can be extremely high and far more costly than most people ever imagine.

Older women are much more likely to reside in nursing homes for longer periods of time. According to the data, some 14.9 percent of women over the age of 85 are in nursing homes for five years or longer while only 10.6 percent of long-stay residents are men.

- The national average daily rate for a private room in a nursing home is $240, while a semi-private room is $212 up slightly from $239 and $214 respectively in 2011.
- The national average monthly base rate in an assisted living community rose from $3,477 in 2011 to $3,550 in 2012, and down to $3,500 in 2014.

- The national average daily rate for adult day services is down from $70 per day in 2012 to $65 per day in 2014.
- The national average: hourly rates for home health aides ($20) remained unchanged, while the homemaker hourly rate decreased $20 per hour in 2012 to $19 in 2014.

CONSIDER THE COSTS

If the average stay in a nursing home is 2.7 months (actually, 835 days), and the average cost of a semi-private room is $212, your total cost would be $177,020. You must also factor in your gender, your current health, your life expectancy, your state's average cost, your income and your other monthly expenses. Most importantly consider your family genetics and family history.

CONCLUSION

Too few people plan for their long term care costs. Long term care insurance can be invaluable. Another option is to self fund your long term care. Still others rely on public benefits like Veterans Benefits and Medicaid. Each case is unique. An elder law attorney can help you make the right decisions. Too many people focus exclusively on asset protection. Asset protection is important, but not solely to pass on to your children. Having money means having security. Without money, you have no security and few options. At the same time you do not want to squander your life savings solely for the benefit of your children while placing your own life to the side. We are a Life care planning law firm.

ABOUT THIS BOOK

1

I wrote this book to assist the American public in making informed decisions about long term care for their loved ones. I am an Elder Law Attorney with the law firm of Zacharia & Brown P.C. currently with two offices in southwestern Pennsylvania. This area of the country happens to have one of the largest populations of the elderly in America. For the nearly twenty years I have been practicing in this area, I've seen and heard thousands of clients say the same thing; "I've never done this before!" It can be frightening. The decisions are overwhelming. Many people are concerned about costs. Often people will make a snap decision based upon the experiences of others. Often that decision is for a place that is not appropriate for the individual's care needs.

I wrote this book to help clear the fog. This book is not a replacement for the hiring of an elder law attorney. Rather, this book was written for you to reference before, and after you meet with an elder law attorney. The legal realm of long term care is one of the most complicated and dangerous areas of the law. It is not a place for the do it yourself individual. You are risking everything the applicant and the applicant's spouse owns, and then some. You may even be risking personal liability. There is a law in Pennsylvania called the Filial Responsibility Act. There was a recent case in Pennsylvania where a nursing home sued the child of a resident to pay their bill. The nursing home won that case. If that does not frighten you, then read it again.

Another problem with doing it yourself is that in applying for Medicaid, you cannot and must not presume that the person who will be handling your case, the state caseworker, knows and fully understands the breadth of the law. Over my many years in this field, I am constantly finding caseworkers who do not understand the law. It's not because they are lacking in intelligence. They are lacking in experience and use as their guidance a policy manual that often is in direct contravention of the laws. On hundreds of occasions I've heard caseworkers make statements about eligibility that are completely contrary to the law. When challenged on the issue with written, legal authority, they often back down. This field is complex. The job of the state caseworker is difficult and many of them have very little experience. If you purchased this book to learn how to do it yourself, you are advised otherwise.

Remember also that for the vast majority of cases, I would say 95% of them, there is spend down involved. The first and most allowable expense in spend down is the legal fee. Many of my clients have stated after the application was completed and they were found eligible, that they did not fully under-stand that concept. They've asked me, "If I can hire an elder law attorney and use funds that I would otherwise spend on a nursing home, why wouldn't I hire someone? Why doesn't everyone hire an attorney to help them?" The only reason I can think of is that they do not understand that concept. You're not saving a dime by trying to do things alone.

This book contains three essential areas as stated in its title: Finding, Getting and Paying for Good Long Term Care. We begin by discussing the maze that is long term care. We then delve into home care options, the differences among the residency options including independent living, assisted living and nursing homes. The latter two are often confused among those unfamiliar with the field.

The second area, getting good care, provides an understand-ing of the tools used to measure the capacity and abilities of an individual called the activities of daily living (ADLs) and the instrumental activities of daily living (IADLs). This is fol-lowed with an explanation of hospice and palliative care and a listing of the federal nursing home resident's rights.

The final area is on paying for that care. We will cover the essentials of Medicare, Medicare HMOs, Medi-Gap plans and Medicare coverage of nursing home stays. Following that, we look into the different benefit plans available to help someone pay for their care. There are the U.S. Department of Veterans Affairs programs and the national Medicaid program. We discuss these programs at length. These are the primary pro-grams utilized by elder law attorneys to help their clients obtain benefits to pay for care. In addition, we will touch upon some other unique methods of utilizing your personal resources and your family resources to obtain care.

In Chapter 15 we then discuss planning ahead and the need for having the proper legal documents in place to protect yourself and your loved ones. In today's world, a world where taxes take less of your money (at death) and where long term care can take more (in fact everything), your estate plan MUST address long term care issues. The vast majority of estate plans do not.

Finally, we showcase for you some of our software applications and smart phone / tablet computer apps. We've developed an app for locating nursing homes and viewing the current Medicare ratings. Visit our website www.GoodLTC.com. Our software applications and apps are available in several places. For smart phones and tablet apps, they are available in the iTunes Store and Google Play.

THE LONG TERM CARE MAZE

2

Preparing for the possible costs of future impairment and long-term care is, regrettably, a task that everyone faces as they age. Loss of a person's ability to function day to day is a natural part of the aging process, and those losses become more severe as people get older. Twenty percent of America's elderly (those age 85 and older) are what some people call the "oldest old." Among this group, over half of them have physical or mental impairments and require long-term care—the personal assistance that enables impaired people to perform daily routines such as eating, bathing, and dressing.

AGING AND LONG-TERM CARE

Impaired people who need long-term care usually need it for a long time—in many cases, until they die. But people may also use the same kinds of services constituting long-term care for relatively short periods, such as during convalescence from a hospitalization or from an injury or illness. That characteristic of long-term care services tends to complicate an understanding of the issues related to long-term care financing.

For example, health insurers cover certain long-term care services, such as home health care, to aid beneficiaries in recovering from specific medical events. But they generally do not cover long-term care services that are needed because of either nonspecific causes related to aging or as a result of chronic, or "long-term," impairment.

When the elder's needs for long-term care can no longer be met either inside the home or without the intervention of paid providers, the elder enters, as we like to say, "the long-term care system." (As we call it here, "the maze.") The elder, and the elder's family, are now embarking on an arduous journey through murky, treacherous waters.

People begin their journey with the observation that the current system in our country for addressing long-term care is a non-system, a hodgepodge of services that fails to meet the needs of the elderly and disabled in the variety of long term care settings. It is economically inefficient and it fails to assure the quality of services that are provided.

The "system" does not fund most long-term care at all, or sporadically, or requires people to "spend down" to obtain eligibility; and the system provides home health care in a hodgepodge fashion. Medicare includes gaps in coverage, especially outpatient prescription medication. For people who need chronic care at home, almost no funding is available to help them in the day-to-day self-management of their illness. As a consequence, the long-term care financing system is biased in favor of providing long-term care in an institutional setting, which usually means a nursing home.

Currently, elderly people finance long-term care services from a variety of sources including private resources—personal savings, care donated by friends and family, and long-term care insurance—and with assistance from public programs such as Medicaid and Medicare.

LIMITED MONEY, LIMITED BENEFITS

Underlying the set of decisions a person makes in preparing financially for future long-term care needs is the availability of publicly funded programs for long-term care, primarily Medicare and Medicaid, and, for some people, veteran's benefits. Medicare does not cover long-term care per se but has become a de facto long-term care financier through its coverage of care in skilled nursing facilities (following hospitalization), its home health care benefit, and, increasingly, its hospice benefit.

Medicaid is the dominant public insurance program for long-term care. Not only does it cover the care of people with very low income, but its eligibility rules permit middle-income people—even seniors whose income in retirement leaves them fairly comfortable—to qualify for coverage by exhausting, or "spending down," their income and assets.

HOME AND COMMUNITY-BASED CARE

The government pays very few benefits to help someone remain in his or her own home for as long as possible, few as well for persons who decide to move into an assisted-living residence, in which they receive assistance with activities of daily living, such as bathing, dressing, food preparation, and the like. Rarely does the government pay the cost of this care. The legislature has decided this type of care is personal care, not health care.

MEDICARE AND HEALTH CARE

Some people think that Medicare pays for long-term care. Medicare pays for health care, not personal or custodial care. For example, Medicare provides limited benefits for short stays in skilled nursing facilities. Hospitals are under increasing pressure to shorten inpatient stays under Medicare's hospital payment system. Patients who are not ready to go home may instead be discharged to skilled nursing facilities. As a result, most nursing home residents either stay for a short period of time on Medicare skilled care or exhaust the benefit during the course of their stay.

MEDICAID AND NURSING HOME CARE

For persons who have to have nursing home care, the legislature has likewise decided this type of care is personal care, not health care. Most nursing home residents begin their stay on skilled nursing care (which is health care, paid for by Medicare and health insurance), and then are taken off skilled and put on intermediate care (which is long-term care, paid for privately, with long-term care insurance, and Medicaid).

Despite the costs, there are advantages to paying privately for nursing home care. The foremost is that it may be easier to get into a nursing home. There are a few nursing homes that do not accept Medicaid residents and only accept residents who are private pay. For a resident who resides in a nursing home that does not accept Medicaid, getting admitted to a Medicaid-certified facility may be difficult. Planning for Medicaid eligibility may therefore limit choices among nursing homes.

FINDING GOOD CARE

3

In order to Find and Get good care, one needs to understand what options are available. That is the basis and reason for this book's existence. This book is a concise reference source that will help you understand your options. Many times we've experienced people requiring a certain level of care and not receiving it because they are either beyond the capabilities of the facility they've chosen or the facility provides more than they need. You need to find the facility or program that can provide for your loved one's needs, in an environment he or she is comfortable. The ability to provide the correct level of care is important, but equally so is putting your loved one in a facility where they can make friends and feel comfortable.

RANGE OF OPTIONS

There is a range of options from at home caregivers to skilled nursing homes. In between there are independent living retirement communities and assisted living facilities and a number of other facilities that specialize in such fields like memory care. The assisted living facilities, known as personal care homes in some states, may offer a number of levels of care from the fairly independent individual to the fairly dependent individual. The independent living communities are typically individual apartments with all the amenities, stove, refrigerator, etc. They have a dining facility, activities, shows and other forms of entertainment. Some offer modest assistance with care, primarily assistance with a few of the instrumental activities of daily living. The degree and amount of assistance may vary from place to place.

Moving beyond the independent living communities, there are assisted living or personal care homes. These are typically rooms with community dining in a dining room. Most offer different levels of care and charge an increased monthly fee for higher levels of care.

In exploring personal care homes/assisted living facilities, one of the most important questions to ask is "How many levels of care do you have, and at what point, if any, would you ask a client to leave because of inability to care for that person?" Some facilities cannot handle persons who require a two person transfer, for example, because of not having enough staff to accommodate two person transfers constantly. Other facilities, on the other hand, have Hoyer lifts, and can handle any level of care when it comes to transfers.

If looking for a placement for someone with dementia, a good question to ask is if the direct care workers (CNAs and aides) receive any dementia-specific training. It's just not enough to be able to bathe someone. They need to have the expertise to handle problems with someone's resistance to bathing when they suffer from dementia. The last thing you want is an aide who charges ahead and forces a frightened person to bathe. The direct care workers should be familiar with dementia-specific communication techniques and have training in that area.

Some assisted living facilities are pet-friendly. Perhaps the family cat is the beloved pet of the person needing care. What better piece of home to bring along than that best friend!

Activities are an important part of life for each of us, but especially when living in a facility. Take a hard look at the "activities calendar" that is posted. Do the activities appear to be cookie-cutter activities, or is there an attempt to tailor things to the interests of the client? Ask to speak to the activities director to discuss your loved one's interests/hobbies. Would it be possible to include their hobbies like Mom's quilting, or Dad's model building into the calendar?

When seriously considering placement in a specific facility, ask to have a meal as part of your visit. Satisfying meals are so important to quality of life, from a nutritional standpoint, but also from a quality-of-life standpoint. Would the kitchen be able to provide for special dietary considerations such as diabetic diet, vegetarianism, gluten-free diet?

Moving on, there are the dementia-focused assisted living facilities that specialize in dementia patients. These places have specialized facilities and specially trained employees who are taught how to deal with victims of dementia.

Many of these facilities are for advanced dementia. Care must be taken not to place an individual with light or mild dementia into a facility where the residents all have advanced dementia. Such a placement might be counterproductive.

At the other end of the spectrum there are skilled nursing facilitiess (SNFs). SNFs can be thought of as hospitals without surgery. They have highly skilled, expensive health care personnel on staff 24 hours a day. They also have expensive equipment designed to help their residents get in and out of bed or on and off the toilet.

MOVING CAN BE FRIGHTENING

Consider how frightening it must be to have lost so much in your life: your spouse, your ability to walk perhaps, to take care of yourself, friends passed away, etc. Consider how hard that must be. At the high point of your life you have everything. Think of a hand of cards, each card representing something important in your life, maybe even important items you now take for granted. As life progresses the cards begin to be taken away. First your spouse, then friends, then the ability to move about freely, then the ability to drive, and so forth. Now you are losing the ability to stay in the comfort, safety and security of your own home. Understand and realize that your loved one is feeling that way. I believe that in many cases, once the transition is made, your loved one will be much happier. Too often seniors that remain in their home alone do not receive the socialization that is required for every human being. Taking that step can be frightening, understand that, but also consider how much better it might be for all involved if your loved one enters a facility (or residence) that can care for him or her and where he or she will

16

make friends and have opportunities to go to shows, the casino, shopping and the other activities we sometimes take for granted.

FACILITIES ARE IN THE BUSINESS OF KEEPING THEIR ROOMS FILLED

These facilities, all of them, are in the business of making money. Some are for profit, others are not for profit. In all cases they need to make enough money to pay their monthly bills. If their residents are not happy, they are going to complain to their families and their families will take them elsewhere. The facilities will usually do whatever they can to make the lives of their residents happy and fulfilling. Consider that an assisted living facility has, on average, 10 empty rooms per month. At a rate of say $4,000 a month, they are losing a half a million dollars a year. Most of them will do much to try to create a safe, friendly, warm and enjoyable environment for their residents. They will have trips to the casino, to shows, to the outlet shops, and more on a weekly basis. Some even have happy hour.

COMPARISON SHOP

Affordability and proximity to friends and family are important. Listed below are some questions you might want to ask, consider and compare for each facility. See our website for more tools.

When you are reviewing facilities for your loved one, here are some questions you should ask and compare:
- Is the nursing home Medicaid-certified?
- Does the nursing home have the level of care needed?
- Does the nursing home have a bed available?

- Does the nursing home offer specialized services, such as a special unit for care for a resident with dementia, ventilator care, or rehabilitation services?
- Is the nursing home located close enough for friends and family to visit?
- Are the residents clean, well groomed, and appropriately dressed for the season or time of day?
- Is the nursing home free from overwhelming unpleasant odors?
- Does the nursing home appear clean and well kept?
- Is the temperature in the nursing home comfortable for residents?
- Does the nursing home have good lighting?
- Are the noise levels in the dining room and other common areas comfortable?
- Is smoking allowed? If so, is it restricted to certain areas of the nursing home?
- Are the furnishings sturdy, yet comfortable and attractive?
- Does the relationship between the staff and residents appear to be warm, polite, and respectful?
- Does the staff wear name tags?
- Does the staff knock on the door before entering a resident's room? Do they refer to residents by name?
- Does the nursing home offer a training and continuing education program for all staff?
- Does the nursing home check to make sure they don't hire staff members who have been found guilty of abuse, neglect or mistreatment of residents; or have a finding of abuse, neglect, or mistreatment of residents in the state nurse aid registry?
- Is there a licensed nursing staff 24 hours a day, including a Registered Nurse (RN) present at least 8 hours per day, 7 days a week?

- Will a team of nurses and Certified Nursing Assistants (CNAs) work with me to meet my needs?
- Do CNAs help plan the care of residents?
- Is there a person on staff who will be assigned to meet my social service needs?
- If I have a medical need, will the staff contact my doctor for me?
- Has there been a turnover in administration staff, such as the administrator or director of nurses, in the past year?
- Can residents have personal belongings and furniture in their rooms?
- Does each resident have storage space (closet and drawers) in his or her room?
- Does each resident have a window in his or her bedroom?
- Do residents have access to a personal phone and television?
- Do residents have a choice of roommates?
- Are there policies and procedures to protect residents' possessions, including lockable cabinets and closets?
- Are exits clearly marked?
- Are there quiet areas where residents can visit with friends and family?
- Does the nursing home have smoke detectors and sprinklers?
- Are all common areas, resident rooms, and doorways designed for wheelchair use?
- Are handrails and grab bars appropriately placed in the hallways and bathrooms?
- Do residents have a choice of food items at each meal? (Ask if your favorite foods are served.)
- Can the nursing home provide for special dietary needs (like low-salt or no-sugar-added diets)?
- Are nutritious snacks available upon request?

- Does the staff help residents eat and drink at mealtimes if help is needed?
- Can residents, including those who are unable to leave their rooms, choose to take part in a variety of activities?
- Do residents have a role in planning or choosing activities that are available?
- Does the nursing home have outdoor areas for resident use? Is the staff available to help residents go outside?
- Does the nursing home have an active volunteer program?
- Does the nursing home have an emergency evacuation plan and hold regular fire drills (bed-bound residents included)?
- Do residents get preventive care, like a yearly flu shot, to help keep them healthy?
- Does the facility assist in arranging hearing screenings or vision tests?
- Can residents still see their personal doctors? Does the facility help in arranging transportation for this purpose?
- Does the nursing home have an arrangement with a nearby hospital for emergencies?
- Are care plan meetings held with residents and family members at times that are convenient and flexible whenever possible?
- Has the nursing home corrected all deficiencies (failure to meet one or more state or Federal requirements) on its last state inspection report?

VISIT EACH FACILITY

While you're visiting the nursing home, ask a member of the resident council if you can attend a resident council or family council meeting. These councils are usually organized and managed by the residents or the residents' families to address concerns and improve the quality of care and life for the resident.

If you're able to go to a meeting, ask a council member the following questions and take notes:

- What improvements were made to the quality of life for residents in the last year?
- What are the plans for future improvements?
- How has the nursing home responded to recommendations for improvement?
- Whom does the council report to?
- How does membership on the council work?
- Who sets the agendas for meetings?
- How are decisions made (for example, by voting, consensus, or one person makes them)?

VISIT AGAIN

It's a good idea to visit the nursing home a second time. It's best to visit a nursing home on a different day of the week and at a different time of day than your initial visit. Staffing can be different at different times of the day and on weekends.

MEDICARE'S COMPARE DATABASE

On a monthly basis, Medicare updates their data on over 15,000 nursing homes across the country. They rate these facilities on several categories such as staffing, quality of care, quality of nursing, complaints lodged, survey infractions, and more. In our apps, **SNF Finder** and **SNF Compare**, we make accessing the COMPARE database easy. Visit our website www.GoodLTC.com for more information or go to the iTunes Store or Google Play.

CARE AT HOME

4

This is the number one desire of almost everyone, to be able to continue to live in the comfort of your own home and receive care at home. When this is possible, it is mostly a good thing for everyone involved. Mostly, you ask? Yes. Most of the time it is a good option. However I have had a very large number of clients who, once they moved into a personal care home or assisted living facility, came to like and enjoy it. There is a strong social element to these places that the person does not get at home. If you look at the business model of an assisted living facility, you can understand it better. These places have a set number of rooms. Let's say one has 50 rooms. They charge $4,000 a month. That is revenue of $200,000 a month. If there are five empty rooms, the owners are losing $20,000 a month. Over a one-year period that is a loss of nearly a quarter of a million dollars. How can they prevent the rooms from being empty? By making their residents comfortable and happy. That is the key. If it is a place where the residents are watched over like small children but never given the opportunity to play and find enjoyment, they will want to leave and many will do so. On the other hand, if the staff and ownership goes out of their way to make the living experience enjoyable, their residents will want to stay. Many of my clients, once there, enjoy the companionship of others their age. They also enjoy all of the activities that take place, such as trips to the movies, going out to dinner, trips to the outlet shops, trips to shows, trips to the casino, entertainers coming into the facility, and old stand bys like Bingo. My point is that there is a socialization element to assisted living facilities that people often do not get at home. Don't forget that.

Back to home care: take a look at the resources in Chapter 7. Look at the ADLs (Activities of Daily Living) and IADLs (Instrumental Activities of Daily Living). If you want to keep your loved one at home, you should take a look at these listings. Can the loved one manage these independently? Will there be someone available to help the loved ones with the management of these ADLs and IADLs when the loved one cannot perform them on his or her own? Also look at the need for another's presence. Can the loved one ever be alone? If he or she cannot, will there be someone available at all times in the home? For those times when the person cannot be alone and there will be no one available to care for him or her, is there somewhere he or she can go?

ADULT DAY CARE

Almost every community has a number of adult day care facilities. These are typically in a community center, a church or some other public gathering place. Adult day care is a place where you can take your loved one in the morning and the people at the center will watch over him or her, have some activities, be fed, and ready for pick up in the afternoon. It can be a good alternative to assisted living, particularly for a married couple where one is healthy and able to care for his or her spouse in the evening but needs time to take care of himself or herself during the day.

PACE PROGRAMS

The Program for All inclusive Care for the Elderly (PACE) is covered in detail in another part of this book. To many, PACE is adult day care, and it is that. They provide social activities and lunch. But it is much more. PACE programs are generally for those individuals who are nursing home eligible but are able to reside in their home because another lives with them and is able to look after them and care for them, particularly at night. Typically with a PACE program, the program's van picks up the residents in the morning and take them to their center. At the center they receive physical and occupational therapies, have their drugs managed, and they are seen by the program's physicians who become their primary physician. There is a much stronger care element and there is a medical element that is not provided at adult day care. PACE programs are generally funded by Medicaid and the recipients are Medicaid recipients. However most also accept private pay. If you are a Pennsylvanian, the PACE I refer to here is completely unrelated to the PACE prescription drug program provided through Pennsylvania lottery revenues. In Pennsylvania they are known as the LIFE programs, Living Independently For Elders.

HOME CAREGIVERS

Home caregivers can be personal friends or acquaintances. They can also be people provided through a service to which you subscribe. There are many such companies in all parts of the country. For an hourly rate a caregiver will come to your home and provide care. There is usually no medical care provided except that they will make sure that the individual is taking their medication as prescribed.

In most states, certainly in Pennsylvania, there is a Medicaid funded program that provides payment to individuals to help pay for the cost of home caregivers. The same basic rules apply as they do for PACE programs. The person must be nursing home eligible but able to stay in their home because there are others in the home to look after the individual when the caregivers are not present. Pennsylvania's program is called the PDA (Pennsylvania Department of Aging) Waiver Program. You will see the word *Waiver* often in long term care. Waiver typically applies to programs that are funded by Medicaid or the Social Security Administration but do not follow the traditional Medicaid rules that the states are required to follow. The state files a request for a waiver (waiving the following of federal law) for a particular program the state wishes to introduce. This is common practice by most all of the states and there are many waiver programs in each state. For our purposes, the waiver part is essentially that the dollars are spent on an elderly person, not in a nursing home but in their own home.

Veterans benefits are another source of funds for receiving care at home. If you have an eligible veteran and have an agreement with a caregiver individual or company to provide a set amount of care giving to a loved one for a particular amount, you may be eligible to obtain funds from the VA. Refer to Chapter 12 on VA benefits eligibility.

Family members are another source of care giving. Rather than pay a company or someone else, if you have a loved one, a child or someone close to you able and willing to provide the level of care that you need, you can hire that person, that child, to be your caregiver. Typically the agreement to provide the care should be in writing for two reasons. A) To obtain benefits from the Veterans Administration (where applicable) and/or B) to prove that the money was for services and not a gift if you need to apply for Medicaid within five years for the date of payment. For more information see the section on Gifting in Chapter 13.

5 RESIDENCE OPTIONS

Think of residency options as a spectrum beginning with home on the left and a nursing home on the far right. From home there are independent living residences, then personal care homes and multiple flavors of what are termed assisted living facilities, then memory care facilities for people with dementia and then finally, the skilled nursing facility. As you move from left to right, the amount of care required increases, as does the price.

INTRODUCTION

Every state in this country has their own way of doing things. Each provides different forms and places for care. The following is a general overview of the most common forms. Your state may have other forms of residency and programs. Your elder law attorney will be helpful and knowledgeable about your state's places and programs.

PRIVATE CAREGIVERS

Many people hire their own caregiver. There are people who, for a fee, will help take care of your loved one. Many of them are paid in cash. The benefit is that these people are usually less expensive than an agency. They are also someone whom you know and feel comfortable with. The downside is that the person is typically not bonded and has little training. Frankly, it's riskier because this person is actually an employee of yours. You are legally responsible for payroll taxes and deductions as well as workers' compensation insurance. This may surprise many of you but it can happen and does happen. The price of that person is lower but the risks are greater. If you hire someone, pay them in cash and they get hurt, you may end up paying a workers' compensation claim. That is a rather large risk to be taking.

CAREGIVER AGENCIES

Caregiver agencies are a form of staffing agency that provide individuals to aid elderly and disabled individuals with the activities of daily living and the instrumental activities of daily living. While agencies are usually more expensive than private caregivers, there are many benefits. All of the hiring and firing is done by the agency. Caregivers are screened and supervised by the agency. If a caregiver gets ill, a backup is usually available. The agency does all of the background checks and has insurance bonds for their workers. Finally, there is no question that when you hire an agency, they are the employer, not you. In addition, most of these agencies provide the on-going training to their employees.

ADULT DAY CARE CENTERS

Adult day care centers offer therapeutic programs of health services and social activities such as leisure activities, self-care training, rest, nutritional services, and respite care for a portion of a day. Many of these are sponsored by a local charity or religious institution. Some nursing homes also provide adult day care services. They do not offer any medical services.

INDEPENDENT LIVING (RETIREMENT COMMUNITIES)

Sometimes there is very little difference between an apartment building and a residential retirement community. The name of the location is usually telling. Independent living locations typically will inform you that the place is a retirement community for older people. Everyone has their own apartment complete with all living facilities such as a kitchen, bathroom, bedroom, etc. They also limit who may reside at the location. Typically the residents must be age 60 or older. Many amenities are also included. There may be limited care giving available when needed. There are almost always social functions and activities such as a bus to the outlet shops, mall, casino, shows and the like. Unlike someone in an assisted living facility, the resident of an independent living establishment must be independent and able to live on one's own.

PROGRAM OF ALL INCLUSIVE CARE FOR THE ELDERLY (PACE)

The Program of All-Inclusive Care for the Elderly (PACE) provides comprehensive long term services and supports to Medicaid enrollees. You can think of a PACE facility as a Medicaid benefit adult day care that provides medical and care services. PACE is usually for an individual who is nursing home eligible but is able to live at home because they live with someone who is able to watch them at night and on weekend. I've found the PACE program to be invaluable to a married couple where one is ill and the other healthy. They do not want to be separated but the healthier spouse needs time during the day to care for himself or herself as well as the household. When you join a PACE program, you use their health care physicians and personnel. The center where the individual spends the day provides medication management, therapies and social activities. You get picked up in the morning and dropped off at home before dinner.

Individuals can join PACE if they meet certain conditions:
- Age 55 or older
- Live in the service area of a PACE organization
- Eligible for nursing home care
- Be able to live safely in the community

The PACE program becomes the sole source of services for Medicare and Medicaid eligible enrollees. Individuals can leave the program at any time.

Home Health Agencies

Home health agencies deliver health and medical services and medical supplies through visits to private homes, assisted living facilities (ALFs), and adult family care homes. Some of the services include nursing care, physical therapy, occupational therapy, respiratory therapy, speech therapy, home health aide services, and nutritional guidance. Medical supplies are restricted to drugs and biologicals prescribed by a physician. Along with services in the home, an agency can also provide staffing services in nursing homes and hospitals. Home health agencies are required to be licensed and inspected by the state of Florida.

ASSISTED LIVING FACILITIES (PERSONAL CARE HOMES)

I will use the term Assisted Living Facility, or ALF to denote any form of residence that is more than independent living but less than a nursing home. In Pennsylvania an ALF is a form of residence but the preferred legal form is Personal Care Home. As with most everything else in long term care, each state has its own naming system and programs.

These places provide 24-hour supervision, assistance, meals, and health care services in a home-like setting. Services include help with eating, bathing, dressing, toileting, taking medicine, transportation, laundry, and housekeeping. Social and recreational activities also are provided. ALF services vary greatly in the types of residents served. For example, some accept residents who need assistance in bathing, while others do not. All ALFs are required to be licensed and inspected by the state.

Of all of the housing and residence options, assisted living facilities are the most complex. At one end of the spectrum you have living at home or living independently. At the other end of the spectrum is the skilled nursing facility where an individual requires around the clock supervision. There is a wide area in between where an individual may need just a bit more care than they can get at home through to the individual who is borderline in need of skilled nursing. There are assisted living facilities that provide services to meet certain levels of care. Some, for example, specialize in memory care and dementia patients. Other facilities do not specialize in that area. Finding the right place can be challenging. That is why I suggest that you contact a life care planning law firm.

These law firms (members of LCPLFA.org) employ individuals termed elder care coordinators or elder care advocates. One of the jobs of the elder care coordinator is to know about all of the various long-term care facilities in their geographic area. The elder care coordinator will have a good grasp on these places and will help you find the appropriate place. An appropriate place is one that meets the needs of the individual, is in close proximity to the family, and is a place the individual can afford.

Because this is a major change for an individual, it can sometimes be helpful if you find a place that meets the above criteria but also has a resident there that your loved one knows. It's like going away from home. It's always helpful to go somewhere where you have a friend.

Some states provide Medicaid coverage for ALF residents. Others do not. Veterans eligible for Aid & Attendance can receive a substantial monthly amount from the VA to help cover the costs of the ALF.

ASSISTED LIVING FACILITY – UNDERSTANDING LEVELS OF CARE

In order to understand assisted living facilities, you need to understand the concept of levels of care. I use phrase assisted living facility (or ALF) throughout this book to mean a facility for the care of older persons that offers more care than an independent living facility, but less than a skilled nursing facility. Some of these ALFs specialize in dementia care, others do not. The cost of care is dependent on the level of care the individual requires. If you are looking into an ALF, make sure you thoroughly understand the cost structure.

RESIDENCE OPTIONS

Some ALFs have a monthly rate and a separate level of care cost. When you hear the monthly rate, you will want to inquire whether that is the full amount. Often times level of care costs are separate. Most ALFs have three or four levels of care. A higher level of care will result in higher monthly payments. In addition to the monthly rate and the level of care cost, there are often charges on a per usage or individual cost. These include such items as incontinence care and medication management. Pricing structures that incorporate levels of care as well as a la carte services can be very complicated, so ask specific questions before signing an agreement.

Facilities that use levels of care do so to simplify their pricing structures. Once a resident requires a certain amount or kind of care, the costs increase. This avoids a constant reassessment of costs every time a resident's needs change. Levels of care are also convenient for the consumer: you know the pricing up front, and can avoid feeling "nickeled-and-dimed" every time a change occurs in care needs.

GUIDELINES IN LEVEL OF CARE DETERMINATION
How the levels of care are determined varies from facility to facility. Some facilities use a point system to determine a resident's required level of care. No cost-of-care fee applies if the resident is considered independent and doesn't require any help. This can also apply to residents who only need verbal instructions to complete the activities of daily living (ADLs). Residents who do require care are assessed prior to moving into the facility. The components that typically determine the level of care a resident requires are listed below.

BATHING

There are two factors here that are reviewed; (1) whether the person requires help showering or bathing and (2) how often they require it. For example, a resident who needs help washing and setting her hair on a weekly basis would require a lower level of care than a resident who requires help with all bathing activities.

DRESSING

Dressing and bathing are two of the most difficult ADLs to manage independently for elderly individuals. An ALF will want to know if a resident can dress him or herself without assistance. Dressing includes not just the ability to get into and out of clothing, it also includes the ability to choose appropriate dress wear given the current weather and season.

GROOMING

Grooming includes activities such as brushing one's hair and teeth, and shaving for men. This means not only being physically able to do it, but also remembering to do so daily or on an as-needed basis.

TRANSFERRING AND MOBILITY

ALFs need to determine how much help a new resident needs in getting around: this includes walking as well as moving from a seated to a standing position. Someone at the high end of the needs level might need a Hoyer lift to be transferred. Lower levels of care could mean that a resident only requires minimal assistance with walking or help moving to his or her wheelchair. At move-in, most assisted living facilities require residents to be able to walk into the facility without assistance from another person (using a mobility aid such as a walker is okay).

CONTINENCE

A resident who is able to manage his or her incontinence without assistance (e.g., a resident who is able to change his or her own liner or diaper) shouldn't have incontinence factored into the costs of care. Residents who require help with their supplies are typically charged. Higher levels of care include residents who exhibit behavioral issues around their incontinence; for example, a resident who refuses to let aides change his or her diapers.

It is not uncommon for facilities to price incontinence care according to an individual resident's needs, rather than incorporating the cost into the levels of care.

CAREGIVERS

A resident who requires care from multiple caregivers simultaneously is likely to be assessed at a higher level. These would include situations where a resident needs a high level of pain management, and a resident is combative when receiving assistance in bathing or having his or her diaper changed. Other examples include residents who have a tendency to wander or leave the facility, residents who are at a very high risk for falls, and residents who require assistance with physical therapy exercises.

FEEDING

Residents who require feeding assistance can fall into all levels of care. The lowest level includes residents who can feed themselves, but need help cutting up food into bite-sized pieces. Higher levels of care might require a caregiver to be present during all mealtimes, either because the resident is physically unable to eat independently or because he or she is at risk for choking. Some residents may be placed at a higher level of care if they have issues with consuming or hoarding food items that present a dietary, safety or medical hazard.

MEDICATION

Difficulty in administration, number taken, and frequency taken are all components that go into determining the care level required for medication management. Lower levels of care provide assistance in keeping prescriptions filled and supervising or administering medications taken orally or in an inhaled form. Higher levels of care are for residents who require help with injectable medications and for those who require nursing supervision. Some facilities also place residents who require advanced medication management on a higher level of care. For example, even if all of a resident's medications are taken orally and do not require an injection, he or she may be placed at a higher level of care. Usually this will occur when a facility has a specified number of medications, such as six or seven, that determines the threshold.

LAUNDRY

Laundry service is sometimes included in the monthly rate, but sometimes it's charged separately. Every facility has a different policy so make sure to ask.

DEMENTIA

One of the more common determinants for higher levels of care is a resident with Alzheimer's or dementia since they usually require a higher level of care. Since dementia tends to be progressive, these residents will need to be reassessed regularly. Most facilities determine a resident's needs by considering the following criteria:

1. **Diagnosis:** Has the resident been diagnosed with dementia? If so, how severe is it?
2. **Behavior:** Does the resident exhibit combative or inappropriate behaviors?
3. **Elopement:** Does the resident wander and is at risk to suddenly leave the facility?
4. **Monitoring:** Does the resident need to be watched very often, or are a few daily checks sufficient-such as in the morning, evenings and a few times throughout the day? Some facilities have devices to track dementia residents, which can help reduce the workload on caregivers, and potentially the cost for consumers.

HOSPICE

Hospice services emphasize comfort measures rather than aggressive curative treatment. Palliative care is the term used for hospice. Hospice is usually not a place but a program. Hospice provides a coordinated program of professional services, including pain control and counseling for patients who have a prognosis of six-months or less to live. Counseling and support for the family members and friends of the terminally ill patient are also provided. Hospice services are predominately provided in the patient's home. However, the services are also available in ALFs and nursing homes. Hospice providers are required to be licensed and inspected by the state. See Chapter 8 for more information on Hospice and Palliative Care.

NURSING HOMES

A nursing home provides nursing care, personal care, and custodial care to people who are ill or physically infirm. I once heard of a nursing home referred to as a hospital without a surgery center. That's not a bad rendition of a definition. Nursing homes are freestanding, which means that they are not part of a hospital. Some nursing homes are part of a continuing care retirement community (CCRC) and are governed through special contracts. I think of nursing homes as providing restorative therapies or as places where custodial care is provided. Many people are in nursing homes in order to receive physical and occupational therapies to improve and return home. Others are past the point where they are able to return home. Those individuals receive only custodial care.

How can you tell if a place is a nursing home versus an assisted living facility? One way is by the daily or monthly costs. Much more often than not, a nursing home will be double the price of an assisted living facility.

MEMORY CARE FACILITY

These facilities specialize in care for residents who suffer from some form of dementia. They provide additional protections such as a secured facility so that the resident is unable to wander off. Memory care facilities are sometimes freestanding locations, other times they are a part of a senior living community, assisted living facility or a nursing home. They tend to cost more than an assisted living facility. Some nursing homes specialize in dementia while others may not accept dementia patients.

SKILLED NURSING UNITS

Skilled Nursing Units (SNUs) are based in hospitals. They typically provide only short term care and rehabilitation services. Some SNUs are located inside the hospital, and some are located in a separate building. The skilled nursing unit is licensed as part of the hospital.

Continuing-Care Retirement Communities (CCRCs)

Continuing Care Retirement Communities, also called Life-Care Communities, offer different levels of care based on the needs of the individual or couple. The care level ranges from an independent living apartment or house to skilled nursing in an affiliated nursing home. CCRC residents are guaranteed care for the rest of their lives. The CCRC residents move from one setting to another based on their needs but continue to remain a part of their CCRC community. Many Continuing Care Retirement Communities have an entrance fee prior to admission as well as a monthly charge. AHCA licenses and inspects the nursing facilities, assisted living facilities, or home health agencies that may be part of a CCRC. The Department of Financial Services regulates the CCRC contracts.

Waiver Programs

One of the most complex areas of long term care is the waiver program. As of this writing there were over 300 elderly waiver programs in the U.S. Waivers are programs that the states can use to test new or existing ways to deliver and pay for health care services in Medicaid and the Children's Health Insurance Program (CHIP). A waiver program for purposes of long term care is a program where an individual can receive care in the home that is paid for by Medicaid. Much like the PACE program, the waiver programs require the person to be nursing home eligible yet able to live in their home because someone is present who can look after the individual in the evening and on weekends. There are also specialized waiver programs for people with disabilities and for children with disabilities. All are programs paid for by Medicaid.

41

GETTING GOOD CARE

6

THE FACILITY'S ABILITY TO CARE FOR YOUR LOVED ONE

Take the time to review the places available for your loved one. Take some time and review their ability to perform the ADLs and IADLs. Comment on each and take that document to some of the facilities in the area. Allow them to review the document and comment on their ability to provide care for your loved one. One of the more difficult placements can be the individual who suffers from dementia and is an elopement risk. An elopement risk is someone who suffers from dementia and may want to take a walk out of the building not knowing where they are. Some facilities specialize in this form of dementia and have locked doors to prevent a resident from wandering away.

ONCE YOU'VE FOUND THE RIGHT PLACE

Getting good care is a function, first, of finding the right place. Finding that place that can provide the level of care needed, in an environment that is conducive to your loved one's well being, that has the resources available, and employees who care, those are some of the main features of getting good care.

FACTORS TO CONSIDER

Once you've found the right place, now what? What can you do to help make certain that your loved one gets appropriate attention and care? That is not an easy task. The goal here is to give you some ideas.

EXPECT GOOD CARE, AND REWARD IT

It's human nature. Reward someone when they do things you want them to do. Be a good tipper. Your loved one is a reflection of you. The staff that cares for your loved one are usually caring people who are working a job and have problems of their own in their lives. Tell them what your loved one wants. Ask them to provide extra special care for your loved one. Then bring a gift every so often. Ask a staff member who watches your loved one to keep an eye on them, to check on that skin lesion and make sure it is looked after and healed. Then give that staff member something, something of value. Whether it be a cash tip, a gift certificate to a restaurant, or a small box of candy. In most cases, your loved one will be a reflection of you. Your kindness and generosity will be remembered and your loved one treated well because of it. On the other hand, on occasion, you will find an individual who is not well suited for the job they've been hired to do. When positive reinforcement does not work, do not hesitate to take the matter up the line. Life Care Planning attorneys (lcplfa.org) have skilled care personnel called Elder Care Coordinators or Elder

Care Advocates. These people are usually social workers or nurses who work for the law firm. When a family learns of inappropriate care of a loved, the law firm will step in with their advocate bearing the power of the law firm, who knows how to sue, to bring the matter to a successful conclusion. It works well for our firm.

AVOID THE INAPPROPRIAT FACILITY

It is difficult often to find the right place. Some places will tell you that they specialize in dementia care. You really MUST know and understand the nature of dementia. It comes in varying degrees. Some dementia facilities are for people who are quite far-gone. These are people who have had dementia for a number of years and are unable to communicate much, or understand much. If your loved one has a mild case of dementia, placing him or her in such a facility may be a huge mistake. They may become quite irate that they are in such a place. On the other hand they may go downhill faster than they would otherwise. Make sure you understand the nature of your loved one's needs. Life Care Planning law firms are the best equipped to help you make these decisions. They are more important than any other decision you can make on behalf of your loved one.

THE WATCHFUL EYE

It is common sense that the person who has visitors will get better care than those who have few visitors. Visitation is important. A good facility for your loved one must necessarily include a facility that is close enough for family members and friends to visit. While there, see how your loved one is doing. Ask how they've been treated. Make sure that they get the good treatment anyone deserves and expects.

WHEN THINGS GO WRONG

It can be quite trying when you visit your loved one and find that it is the middle of the afternoon and they've not eaten anything yet. Or their diaper is soiled and has been soiled for hours. On occasion this will happen and there is little that can be done to make certain it never happens. But when it happens more often, it is time to take action. We suggest that a letter be provided to the administrator detailing what occurred and demanding, in respectful terms, what actions the facility will take to avoid these occurrences in the future. If you run into a wall and do not get the answers you need and expect, you may want to take the matter up with your local ombudsman. An ombudsman is a mediator of sorts. It is their job to intervene and work with both parties to iron out the differences and reach a conclusion to avoid occurrences in the future.

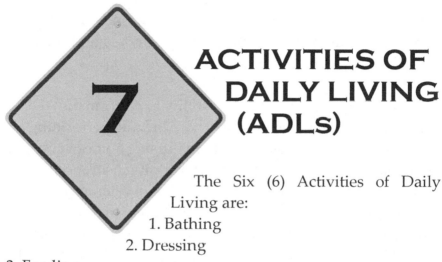

ACTIVITIES OF DAILY LIVING (ADLs)

The Six (6) Activities of Daily Living are:
1. Bathing
2. Dressing
3. Feeding
4. Toileting
5. Continence
6. Transferring (Moving Your Body)

Sometimes you will see Toileting and Continence combined for five activities. For our purposes, we will refer to six. One's ability and the degree of that ability to perform these functions are measured and used throughout the health care industry.

APPLICATION AND USAGE OF ADL MEASUREMENTS

Eligibility for long term care insurance, Medicaid, and other benefit programs have medical requirements as well as financial requirements. In order to make a claim on a long-term care insurance policy, or to be eligible for Medicaid a medical test must be passed. That test is based upon the person's ability to perform the ADLs independently. Most assisted living facilities have stages or levels of care. The costs of care at different levels vary based upon the resident's abilities or inability to perform certain functions independently. To understand these medical requirements, and to truly understand your Long Term Care options, you must first understand the concept of the Activities of Daily Living (ADLs).

An assessment of an individual's ability to perform the ADL is done for any number of reasons. These include performing an assessment for facility placement in a nursing home or assisted living facility, application for long term care insurance, application for benefits including Medicaid and Veterans benefits, etc. When a person receives occupational therapy and/or physical therapy, it is often to assist the person in regaining their ability to perform the ADLs. Think of ADLs as a benchmark. If someone is seeking placement into an assisted living facility, the facility may inquire as to the number of the ADLs the person can perform independently. This way the facility will have a better understanding of whether they are able to meet the needs of the individual seeking placement.

ADLs are defined as "the things we normally do...such as feeding ourselves, bathing, dressing, grooming, work, homemaking, and leisure." National surveys collect data on the ADL status of the U.S. population. While basic categories of ADLs have been suggested, what specifically constitutes a particular ADL in a particular environment for a particular person may vary. There is no real standard set of ADLs. You may hear someone refer to grooming as an ADL. Others may refer to that as personal hygiene. Still others may refer to it as bathing. The concept is essentially the same.

THE INSTRUMENTAL ACTIVITIES OF DAILY LIVING (IADLS)

Instrumental activities of daily living (IADLs) are similar to but go beyond the basic ADLs. IADLs are necessary to allow an individual to live independently in their house or community. These include these abilities:

- Caring of others (including selecting and supervising caregivers)
- Caring of pets
- Child rearing
- Using communication devices
- Managing finances
- Managing and maintaining health
- Preparing meals
- Following safety procedures and emergency responses
- Performing housework
- Taking medications as prescribed
- Managing money
- Shopping for groceries or clothing
- Using transportation within the community

A person in need of support of one or more Activities of Daily Living may be a candidate for assisted living. It may also be the case that an individual who does not need assistance with ADLs may also benefit from the amenities of an assisted living facility, especially when this person needs assistance with one or more IADLs.

A person's ability to perform IADLs is often evaluated by an occupational therapist in the conducting of an assessment. IADLs are generally optional in an assessment because they are tasks that can usually be assigned to another individual.

EVALUATION OF ADLS

There are several evaluation tools, such as the Katz ADL scale, the Lawton IADL scale, and the Bristol Activities of Daily Living scale. Most providers of health care services utilize ADL assessment and evaluations in their practice.

The Katz ADL Index assesses basic activities of daily living. It does not assess the instrumental activities of daily living. Although the Katz ADL Index is sensitive to changes in declining health status, it is limited in its ability to measure small increments of change seen in the rehabilitation of older adults.

The Lawton IADL scale is a questionnaire or interview that takes 10 to 15 minutes to administer and contains eight items. Patients are scored according to their highest level of functioning in that category. A summary score ranges from 0 (low function, dependent) to 8 (high function, independent) for women, and 0 through 5 for men. It should be noted that the scale should not be administered to individuals living in institutions such as long-term care facilities; these older adults typically do not complete their own IADL.

The Bristol Activities of Daily Living Scale (BADLS) is a 20-item questionnaire designed to measure the ability of someone with dementia to carry out daily activities such as dressing, preparing food and using transportion.

ACTIVITIES OF DAILY LIVING (ADLs)

CHOICE OF RESIDENCE AND THE ADL / IADL

As a general rule that has its exceptions, a person's growing need of support of his or her ADLs tends to follow an accumulative pattern. The first ADL, and most often supported, tends to be bathing. After this, a person will also tend to need support in dressing him or herself; next comes toileting, transferring and eating respectively.

This pattern leaves out supported IADLs, which have not been shown to follow such a trend and are supported more often. For example, just under half of residents need assistance in placing or receiving phone calls, and more than three-fourths of residents need at least some assistance in traveling, shopping, taking medication, and managing money.

Care facilities, such as assisted living communities, often use ADL and IADL evaluations of a prospective resident to rate that person's need for support. This is necessary and beneficial because different communities provide different levels of care and ADL evaluations help to ensure the prospective resident is a good fit and will receive the support he or she needs.

COMMUNICATION IS KEY

The Key to getting good care includes communicating your loved one's needs. While you may not be a health care professional, you may be the best person to answer questions about your loved one's abilities to perform ADLs and IADLs. If you are going to have caregivers come into your loved one's home, or if you are going to place your loved one in a facility, those caregivers or facilities operators need to know the degree and level of your loved one's ADLs and IADLs. The software program we are developing at GoodLTC will assist you in providing the facility or caregiver company a complete assessment of your loved one's abilities. Providing them with the information they need regarding your loved one will go a long way towards achieving good, quality care for your loved one. The program simply lists all of the ADLs and IADLs and asks you to rank and comment on each one. You complete the items, print out the report, and provide it to the proposed facilities or caregivers. They will then have the answers to most of the medical questions they will need to be able to provide your loved one with the best care possible. If they review the ADL/IADL document and believe they will not be able to provide your loved one with the kind of care he or she requires, you will know that before ever placing your loved one in that facility. It is never a good idea to move a frail elderly person from place to place. They need, as do we all, a place to call home.

END OF LIFE CARE, HOSPICE & PALLIATIVE CARE

At the end of life, each of our stories will be unique. For some, death will be a long process involving an illness or condition lasting years; for example, Alzheimer's disease. For others, death can come suddenly and unexpectedly. And for many people, the physical body ages, weakens, becomes frail, and eventually fails. One thing is certain: death is inevitable. So the question then becomes, how can we help our loved one experience "a good death"?

A "good death" means different things to different people. For some, it may mean a death that is pain-free and surrounded by loved ones. For others, it may be having the opportunity to spend meaningful time with family, or being able to have those "last words" with the people who mean the most to them. Perhaps a person's last wish is to die peacefully at home. Perhaps someone else would want to be alone or even in a hospital receiving treatment until the end. Certainly each of us is unique; but one common need that we all have is that we want to have our end-of-life wishes to be followed. And each of us wants to be treated with dignity and compassion.

The first step then, is to have the conversation with our loved ones about our last wishes. That is the only way to insure that our dying wishes are followed. Admittedly, it's a very tough topic of discussion and families tend to want to avoid that discussion at all costs. But it is usually a topic that is on everyone's mind anyway when someone is quite ill, but no one will bring it up. It becomes the proverbial "elephant in the room." The family doesn't want to begin the discussion because they don't want to upset the person who is ill. The person who is dying avoids the topic because he or she doesn't want to upset the family. But that puts the dying person in a very lonely place of not being able to talk about their fears, wishes, and concerns. It is so very important to realize that end-of-life care includes helping the dying person cope with the mental and emotional distress often associated with dying. So, have the discussion!

FINDING THE RIGHT END OF LIFE CARE OPTIONS

Beginning with a frank discussion with the family physician would be helpful. The doctor or other health care professional may recommend either hospice or palliative care. What is the difference?

HOSPICE CARE

At some point, curative medical treatment may no longer make sense to continue: it may no longer be effective in treating the disease; there may be no hope of recovery; or the treatment may actually be making the person more uncomfortable. Hospice is appropriate for this situation. The client understands that his or her illness is no longer responding to medical treatment; the illness cannot be cured and its progression cannot be slowed down. The emphasis, then, switches from curative to providing comprehensive comfort care. Attempts to cure the person's illness are stopped. However, it is important to remember that discontinuing the specific treatment to cure the illness does not mean discontinuing all treatment. For example, if a person discontinues chemotherapy for cancer, he or she may still receive medication for hypertension.

Hospice is a philosophy of care...it is not tied to a specific location or setting. Hospice care can be provided wherever the dying person is being cared for at home, in the hospital, nursing home, assisted living facility, or in some cases, in an in-patient hospice facility. People are eligible for hospice if their health care provider feels they have six months or less to live. What happens if someone under hospice care lives longer than six months? If the healthcare provider continues to certify that the person is still close to dying, Medicare/insurance will continue to pay for hospice services.

FOUR GOALS OF HOSPICE

1. Physical comfort involving such things as pain management, breathing problems and shortness of breath, digestive problems such as nausea & vomiting, constipation and lack of appetite, skin irritation, extreme fatigue.
2. Mental & emotional support. Social workers and/or counselors help the patient and family with issues such as anxiety, fear, depression, grieving, etc. They can be an

invaluable resource for both the dying individual as well as the family.

3. Spiritual support. People nearing the end of their lives may have spiritual needs as compelling as their physical needs. A chaplain, rabbi, or minister are available to help the individual with their spiritual needs. This may involve finding peace with unresolved issues, or searching for meaning in their lives, or perhaps helping to end long-standing conflicts within a family.

4. Practical Considerations. Obtaining durable medical equipment and necessary medications, etc. Providing volunteer respite caregivers to give a family a much-needed break for a few hours. Providing caregiver support and education and bereavement after care.

Hospice care provides compassionate comfort care to persons with a life-limiting illness and their loved ones. All services are based on the foundations of dignity and respect for the individual.

PALLIATIVE CARE

Palliative care refers to a comprehensive approach to improving the quality of life for people who are living with potentially fatal diseases. Palliative care is not just for people who are soon to die. It is intended for anyone with chronic, life-limiting illnesses. These include conditions such as heart failure, COPD, Parkinson's disease, renal failure, etc.

Palliative care is a wonderful option, when appropriate. The type of services provided are similar to those found within hospice. Clients can benefit greatly from the comprehensive care provided, with the goal of enhancing the patient's quality of life by providing support, pain control, symptom management, emotional and spiritual counseling, personal care, volunteer support & companionship, art, music & therapeutic touch therapies, and bereavement counseling.

The difference between palliative care & hospice is that the patient can continue with treatments and medical care (e.g. radiation, chemo) in palliative care. The client is not asked to make a choice between treatment and comfort measures. (In hospice care, all aggressive treatment is discontinued and the care is comfort measures only).

Palliative care can be provided at home, in the hospital, a nursing home or in an assisted living facility.

WHO PAYS FOR PALLIATIVE CARE & HOSPICE?
Most major health plans, including Medicare and Medicaid, cover hospice and palliative care services. Coverage generally includes visits by the hospice & palliative care team, medical equipment, such as a hospital bed, wheelchair and oxygen, therapies and medications.

RESIDENTS RIGHTS

9

This chapter highlights the rights of nursing home residents. Residents' rights are part of the federal Nursing Home Reform Law enacted in 1987 in the Social Security Act. The law requires nursing homes to "promote and protect the rights of each resident" and places a strong emphasis on individual dignity and self-determination. Nursing homes must meet residents' rights requirements if they participate in Medicare or Medicaid. The following is an overview of the ways that the law protects residents' rights.

QUALITY OF LIFE

The Nursing Home Reform Law requires each nursing home to "care for its residents in such a manner and in such an environment as will promote maintenance or enhancement of the quality of life of each resident." This requirement emphasizes dignity, choice, and self-determination for residents.

PROVIDING SERVICES AND ACTIVITIES

Each nursing home is required to "provide services and activities to attain or maintain the highest practicable physical, mental, and psychosocial wellbeing of each resident in accordance with a written plan of care which . . . is initially prepared, with participation to the extent practicable of the resident, the resident's family, or legal representative." This means that a resident should not decline in health or well being as a result of the way a nursing facility provides care.

SPECIFIC RIGHTS

The Nursing Home Reform Law legally protects the following rights for nursing home residents:

The Right to Be Fully Informed, including the right to:

1. Be informed of all services available as well as the charge for each service;
2. Have a copy of the nursing home's rules and regulations, including a written copy of resident rights;
3. Be informed of the address and telephone number of the State Ombudsman, State survey agency office, and other advocacy groups;
4. See the State survey reports of the nursing home and the home's plan of correction;
5. Be notified in advance of any plans to change their room or roommate;
6. Daily communication in the resident's language, for example, Spanish;
7. Assistance if they have a sensory impairment.

RESIDENTS RIGHTS

The Right to **Participate in Their Own Care**, including the right to:

8. Receive adequate and appropriate care;
9. Be informed of any changes in their medical condition,
10. Participate in their assessment, care planning, treatment, and discharge;
11. Refuse medication and treatment;
12. Refuse chemical and physical restraints;
13. Review their medical record.

The Right to Make Independent Choices, including the right to:

14. Make independent personal decisions, such as what to wear and how to spend free time;
15. Reasonable accommodation of their needs and preferences by the nursing home;
16. Choose their own physician;
17. Participate in community activities, both inside and outside the nursing home;
18. Organize and participate in a Resident Council or other resident advisory group.

The Right to Privacy and Confidentiality, including the right to:

19. Private and unrestricted communication with any person of their choice;
20. Privacy in treatment and in the care of their personal needs;

21. Confidentiality regarding their medical, personal, or financial affairs.

The Right to Dignity, Respect, and Freedom, including the right to:

22. Be treated with the fullest measure of consideration, respect, and dignity;
23. Be free from mental and physical abuse, corporal punishment, involuntary seclusion, and physical and chemical restraints;
24. Self-determination.

The Right to Security of Possessions, including:

25. Manage their own financial affairs;
26. File a complaint with the State survey and certification agency for abuse, neglect, or misappropriation of their property if the nursing home is handling their financial affairs;
27. Be free from charge for services covered by Medicaid or Medicare.

Rights During Transfers and Discharges, including:

28. Remain in the nursing facility unless a transfer or discharge:
- is necessary to meet the resident's welfare;
- is appropriate because the resident's health has improved and the resident no longer requires nursing home care;
- is needed to protect the health and safety of other residents or staff; or

- is required because the resident has failed, after reasonable notice, to pay the facility charge for an item or service provided at the resident's request;

29. Receive thirty-day notice of transfer or discharge. The notice must include the reason for transfer or discharge, the effective date, the location to which the resident is transferred or discharged, a statement of the right to appeal, and the name, address, and telephone number of the state long-term care ombudsman;

30. A safe transfer or discharge through sufficient preparation by the nursing home.

The Right to Complain, including the right to:

31. Present grievances to the staff of the nursing home, or to any other person, without fear of reprisal;

32. Prompt efforts by the nursing home to resolve grievances;

33. Complain to the survey agency and ombudsman program.

The Right to Visits, including the right to:

34. Immediate access by a resident's personal physician and representatives from the state survey agency and ombudsman programs;

35. Immediate access by their relatives and for others "subject to reasonable restriction" with the resident's permission;

36. Reasonable visits by organizations or individuals providing health, social, legal, or other services.

These rights are set forth in federal law. Unfortunately they do not give any individual the power to file a civil lawsuit against a nursing home for its failure to strictly follow any of these items. However, each facility is licensed and is required to follow these rules. If they do not, speak with your elder law attorney about appropriate recourse.

PAYING FOR CARE

10

A person preparing for possible future long-term care needs has several options from which to choose. One alternative is to "self-insure" by setting aside personal savings and assets and then supplementing those personal resources with the donated, or free, care of family and friends. In fact, the majority of impaired seniors rely solely on donated care and their own savings. The value of donated care probably exceeds that of any other category of long-term care financing but is difficult to quantify in dollar terms.

An individual who self-insures retains maximum flexibility and control over his or her savings and assets but must bear the full financial risk of impairment, which will depend on the extent and duration of functional losses. Significant impairment can leave little, if any, wealth for bequests or other uses.

When it comes to paying the cost of long-term care—whether in a nursing home, assisted-living, or home- and community-based care—there are, therefore, really only two choices: (1) private wealth or (2) public benefits.

These are not mutually exclusive. Seldom will the public pay all costs of someone's care, at least not for an extended period of time. In fact, most public benefits programs in the United States have a cost sharing or co-payment component. For example, Medicare's skilled nursing facility benefit pays all costs for the first 20 days; for the 21st to 100th day, the patient pays a co-payment of $152 per day (2014). Medicaid requires that the nursing home resident pay all of her income to the nursing home, less certain allowable deductions such as the Personal Needs Allowance and payment of medical insurance premium(s).

PRIVATE WEALTH

This consists of the individual's money, his family's money, and borrowed money. It may include what we call "liquid money" such as money in the bank, CDs, and savings bonds; and it may also include "illiquid money," which includes the value of real estate and business interests. It also includes insurance.

It is important to remember that private wealth can be both assets and income. Why is this important? Because disabled or near-disabled persons typically do not need assets (a potful of money); instead, they need an assured income stream to maintain their standard of living. In our planning, the distinction between assets and income is often critical.

Sources of income include Social Security retirement, Railroad Retirement, pension, rents, royalties, immediate annuity payments, interest, dividends, alimony, installment note payments, reverse mortgage payments, line of credit, and earnings from employment.

PUBLIC BENEFITS

Later chapters will discuss these benefits in greater detail. To summarize:

- Medicare: Pays for health care, such as hospital and doctor bills, rehabilitation in a skilled nursing facility, and hospice care.
- Medicaid: Pays for intermediate care in a nursing home, provided that the Medicaid recipient meets minimum assets and income levels and exemptions.
- Medicaid or State Medicaid waiver programs (often called SSI Supplements): Pays for health care for indigent persons.
- Veterans benefits: Pays for health care and some long-term care costs depending upon the facility and the status of the veteran or the veteran's spouse.

LONG TERM CARE INSURANCE

What about Long Term Care Insurance you may ask? I am a proponent of long-term care insurance. It does not, however, pay for the entire cost of a nursing home. Long Term Care Insurance (LTCI) is an insurance contract that will pay the insured a daily, weekly or monthly sum of money once the insured meets the medical requirements. Most often the medical requirements involve an inability to perform two or more of the activities of daily living independently. The insurance company will pay once the exclusion period is over and will pay for as long as the insured is alive, needs care of the level called for in the contract, for as long as the period of time contracted, usually two or more years.

The Exclusion period is usually sixty to ninety days. Basically, once you are eligible to file a claim on the policy, you must wait for the exclusion period before you can be paid on the policy. For many people it is not an issue because Medicare will be making the payment during that time period.

Older LTCI policies are not as clear about what obligates the insurance company to pay. Their definitions were not as clear because there were not facilities called assisted living or personal care homes. More current policies are much clearer. Many will provide coverage or provide coverage at a lesser rate if the insured requires care in an assisted living facility or a personal care home.

There are also home care options. These can be the best policies for many people. You may want to look for a policy that makes payment to you for in home care. Some policies do not cover home care as an option, others do.

When looking for a policy and comparing them, look at such items as;
- Financial stability of the insurance company;
- Home care options;
- Shorter exclusion periods;
- Inflation riders;
- Flexibility in residence options;
- Whether there is a limitation on premium increases;
- Term of coverage; and
- Amount of benefit paid.

Understand that the insurance company will make the payment to you for the amount of coverage. If the policy pays $100 a day, over a 30-day month they will pay $3,000. That, along with your social security, pension and other sources of monthly income may be enough to pay for an assisted living or personal care home. It probably will not be enough to cover a skilled nursing home, which, in Pennsylvania, currently average over $8,766 a month. Still, it will help lessen the monthly drain on your assets.

The biggest problem with LTCI policies are twofold, insurability and cost. Often, when someone is interested in purchasing a LTCI policy, they are older and either the cost of the premiums is too great, or they are not insurable. Often people who, for years had been making payments on their policy stop and let the policy lapse because the rates have gone up far too much to be affordable.

It might be worth your while, if you are younger and in fairly good health to inquire into the benefits and costs of a LTCI policy.

OTHER OPTIONS

While private pay, Medicaid, Medicare and Veterans benefits are the primary sources of funding for care payment, a good elder law attorney will help you discover more imaginative ways of paying for care.

When it comes to the finances of an elderly person of middle class means or less, the family must be ever cognizant of the possibility of an extended stay at a long-term care facility. Although one may be in great health for their age, one simple fall and off to the hospital, then nursing home, they go.

The costs of care are great. If the stay lasts long enough, the individual will be applying for Medicaid. The $5,000 gift the individual made four years ago and the three $3,000 gifts the individual made over the past three years, and all other gifts are now coming back to haunt them all.

See Chapter 13 on gifting for more information on the gifting rules. When these penalties are assessed, you can appeal with the argument that the gifts were not for purposes of obtaining Medicaid but exclusively for other purposes. You may win, or you may not.

A better idea might be to give something in exchange, in exchange for care. A contract whereby a child is given something of value in exchange for assisting with one's care. A capable elder law attorney can help with this. The tool is generally called a Personal Care Agreement and must be properly drafted by an elder law attorney.

While a gift is the giving to someone and not getting something of equivalent value in return, a giving to someone in exchange for their help and assistance with ADLs or IADLs or something else will often be a reason for treating the transfer as something other than a gift.

Review your assets. Do you have a large life insurance policy? Vacation real estate property? These might make good items to transfer in exchange for care or something else of value. If life insurance, the value being given is not the death benefit. The value is the cash value. Thus if you have a $100,000 policy with cash value of $20,000, the transfer value of that policy would be $20,000. That is the value presently and what the owner could get for it from the company. Speak with your elder law attorney about these and other inventive ideas for your case.

MEDICARE PAYMENT

THE ROLE OF MEDICARE IN LONG TERM CARE

One of the biggest (and worst) surprises that face people when a loved one is in a nursing home is to find out that the health insurance they had will not cover the costs of the stay. They are surprised, bewildered, and skeptical. That's the way it is though. This section will give you an idea of how Medicare and its various forms provide coverage in a nursing home.

THE PROBLEM

The problem is that Medicare is an insurance program to help someone get better following an illness. For many elderly people in a nursing home, there is only so much that can be done to help a person improve. There are primarily physical and occupation therapy regimens utilized to assist the person regain their ability to live independently. However, with advanced age comes an advanced inability to manage these therapies. As such, Medicare comes to an end. When it comes to an end is the subject of wide dispute. Historically Medicare coverage ends when the person no longer shows any sign of progress. The family is told that the loved one has "plateaued" and that Medicare (or any form thereof as discussed below) will no longer provide coverage. The family is then informed that the daily cost of care is $250. In Pennsylvania where I practice, the average cost of care is $293.15 per day (2015). That's over $8,900 a month, approximately $107,000.00 a year. There is a strong argument that plateauing is not the proper guideline to determine coverage but that is a legal argument beyond the scope of this book. For more information, visit www.medicareadvocacy.org.

THE FORMS OF MEDICARE COVERAGE
To understand Medicare coverage you must know that there are basically three classifications of coverage:
1. Traditional Medicare,
2. Traditional Medicare with a supplemental policy, and
3. Medicare Advantage (Part C) through an HMO.

TRADITIONAL MEDICARE FOR NURSING HOME CARE
Traditional Medicare provides up to 100 days of coverage in a nursing home. Under any circumstances, after 100 days has passed, coverage ceases. The first twenty (20) days are covered in full. Days 21 through 100 require a co-pay of $157.50 per day. In order to be covered there are these requirements. The individual must have been an inpatient in a Medicare certified hospital for 3 days or more, admitted to a skilled nursing facility within 30 days of discharge, where skilled care is received. Beware! Many hospitals are claiming that an

individual was in the hospital for observation purposes only. Thus, it is possible (and we've seen it occur) that an individual can be in the hospital for more than 3 days, then discharged immediately to a skilled nursing facility, and informed that there is no Medicare coverage. How can this be? The hospital placed the person on observation status. In that capacity, the person was never admitted to the hospital. They were considered to be an outpatient. This is another one of those reasons to make certain that you have a qualified, experienced elder law attorney on your side.

TRADITIONAL MEDICARE WITH A SUPPLEMENTAL OR MEDIGAP POLICY

Those who enroll in a traditional Medicare plan often choose to enroll in a Medicare Supplemental Plan as well, called a Medigap plan, to cover any "gaps" in their Original Medicare plan. Others choose to enroll in Medicare Advantage (HMO) Plans. These plans cover everything in Medicare parts A, B and D, and they also offer many extra benefits.

Medigap plans are offered through many insurance companies around the nation. These plans cover any gaps left by the Original Medicare plan. Medigap plans will pay on healthcare claims after Medicare pays on the claims. Just like any other health insurance plan, Medigap plans have their good points and their not-so-good points. Any healthcare provider that accepts Medicare will accept all Medigap Plans. (i.e. there are no networks, Medicare Supplements are not HMOs or PPOs) You do not ever need a referral to see a doctor or specialist. Medigap plans are standardized (A-N). This means you can compare prices from one company to another and always know you are comparing the exact same coverage. Many of these plans cover the co-pay for days 21 through 100. Generally, premiums are the only out-of-pocket costs throughout the year. Medigap Policies are "Guaranteed Renewable." This means that as long as you continue to pay your premium, you can never lose the coverage. If you move to another city or state, you can take your Medigap policy with you.

DOWNSIDE OF MEDIGAP POLICIES

The average monthly Medigap policy premium is around $150.00. Some Medicare Supplement companies offer big discounts for things such as not using tobacco, or being married, spousal discounts, female discounts and others. Working with an insurance agent can help you find these discounts.

The monthly premium must be paid even if you never visit a doctor or hospital during the year.

Medigap policies do not include prescription drug coverage. You need to get a separate Medicare Part D plan for this.

MEDICARE ADVANTAGE PLANS (HMO COVERAGE)

Medicare Advantage Plans, also known as Medicare Health Plans, MA, Medicare Part C or MAPD plans, provide coverage for everything included in Medicare parts A, B and D, along with many added benefits. They are often offered through companies that provide individual and group plans. There are many different types of MA plans, including HMOs, PPOs and PFFSs.

These plans offer low monthly premiums. The average is $50. They can be offered with "No Monthly Premium" to you because Medicare takes your $99.50 monthly Medicare Part B premium and gives it to the Medicare Advantage Provider. Medicare also pays Medicare Advantage companies additional funds to help cover your Medicare expenses (the money that was deducted from your pay check throughout your working career). The coverage for nursing home care varies widely between these companies. It is important for you to understand how long they provide coverage and what the co-pay is, if any.

Some Medicare Advantage plans include prescription drug coverage. These are called MAPD plans. Some additional benefits such as coverage for dental (routine cleanings), vision (routine checkup), and health club memberships are available through these plans.

DOWNSIDE OF MEDICARE ADVANTAGE PLANS

They are not standardized. There are many different varieties of MA plans. Consumers must carefully review each plan to make sure they know what they are getting. MA plans are not "Guaranteed Renewable." The company can discontinue the plan at the end of any year. You would then need to get another plan for the following year. Doctors can choose not to accept any or all of the MA plans. Even if they accept Medicare, they do not have to accept MA plans. Your primary care physician may accept the plan but a referred specialist may not. The attending physician at the nursing home may not accept coverage from your plan. There is generally more paperwork for the consumer. Many co-pays are a percentage of the Medicare approved amount, which is not known until after the bill has been submitted to the Medicare Advantage provider, so you will be billed for your co-pay at a later date, sometime several months later.

It is very important to investigate all of the available options before choosing a plan. Most Life Care Planning members (www.lcplfa.org) will bring in a Medicare coverage insurance expert to review the coverage of an individual who has entered into a nursing facility or any long-term care facility.

ANNUAL ENROLLMENT VERSUS SPECIAL ENROLLMENT PERIODS.

When an individual enters into a nursing home, they are permitted to change their insurance coverage. This is known as a Special Enrollment Period. When one enters the facility he or she may join a Medicare Advantage Plan or Medicare Prescription Drug Plan, switch from their current plan to another Medicare Advantage Plan or Medicare Prescription Drug Plan, drop their Medicare Advantage Plan and return to Traditional Medicare, and/or drop their Medicare prescription drug coverage.

The reasons to investigate special enrollment might not be immediately obvious at first. When an individual goes to a nursing home, they will typically be changing their primary care provider, receiving their prescriptions from a different pharmacy (one that is under contract with the nursing facility), and obtaining some coverage for skilled care from that facility. If a new resident of a nursing home is going to be there for the foreseeable future, it is important that the person obtain health insurance coverage from the company that provides coverage for these changes.

GENERAL RULES FOR MEDICARE COVERAGE IN A SKILLED NURSING FACILITY

The rules in this section apply to what is called traditional Medicare. If you have a Medicare Advantage (HMO) plan, your rules may vary in numerous ways. Contact your carrier, review your plan, and find out what your coverage may be.

In traditional Medicare, in order to get any coverage whatsoever, the individual must have been hospitalized for three days or more on an in-patient basis and enter a skilled nursing facility within 30 days of discharge from the hospital, where the individual receives skilled care. Coverage will not be for greater than 100 days maximum, the first 20 days are paid in full and there is a co-pay of $157.50 (2014) for days 21 through 100.

LESS THAN 100 DAYS

You may not (and chances are will not) receive the full 100 days. Many people expect coverage for as long as their loved one is in the facility and are shocked and surprised to find out that is not the case. If you have a Medicare HMO, check to see what their requirements are for skilled-care coverage. Often times preapproval is required. It is important that you check with them about coverage as soon as possible. If you have a supplemental plan, the traditional rules apply but some portions may be covered. For example, the co-pay for days 21-100 is often covered by a supplemental plan.

You may hear the term *plateau*. The comment is often made, "Your loved one has plateaued, and the therapies are no longer warranted." For years Medicare nursing facilities because they have reached the conclusion that the therapies are not working or are no longer warranted have discontinued coverage. They claim that Medicare coverage is for improvement only. That is not and was not ever the case. Arguably if a person's condition will worsen if their therapies are discontinued, coverage should be provided. If you are facing this issue and are concerned about your loved one's termination of therapies and Medicaid coverage, you should contact your elder law attorney for assistance and guidance quickly, before the period to appeal ends.

12

VETERANS BENEFITS

BENEFITS FOR VETERANS AND THEIR FAMILIES

The United States Department of Veterans Affairs (VA) offers a broad range of services for veterans of all ages. Unfortunately, some services are underused because many older veterans and their families do not realize these services exist or that they may qualify. They don't apply for VA benefits even though factors such as low income, disability, or wartime service may have made them eligible. The VA Improved Pension program, known generally as Aid & Attendance, is one of the largest providers of benefits for qualified veterans or their surviving spouses for long term care costs. The veteran does not have to have a war-related injury or disability. Nor does the person need to have served overseas. In addition, you do not have to be receiving care in a VA home or facility. Aid & Attendance is one of the largest payers of benefits to many in assisted living facilities or who are receiving care at home. The benefit can be great, over $2,000 a month for a qualified married veteran who is in need of care. You need to view VA benefits in a special way. They are obviously not available to everyone. They are available to qualified veterans or sometimes to the surviving spouse of an otherwise qualified veteran. They are not available to all citizens. As such, they have a special set of rules that they can create, change or remove as the VA sees fit.

GENERAL ELIGIBILITY FOR VA BENEFITS

Eligibility for most VA benefits is based upon discharge from active military service under other than dishonorable conditions. Honorable and general discharges qualify a veteran for most VA benefits. Dishonorable and bad conduct discharges issued by general courts-martial bar VA benefits. VA regional offices can clarify eligibility of prisoners and parolees. Active service means full-time service as a member of the Army, Navy, Air Force, Coast Guard, or as a commissioned officer of the Public Health Service, the Environmental Services Administration or the National Oceanic and Atmospheric Administration.

Women veterans are eligible for the same VA benefits as male veterans. Additional services and benefits for women veterans are gender-specific and include breast and pelvic examinations and other general reproductive health-care services. Preventive health care provided includes counseling, contraceptive services, menopause management, Pap smears and mammography. Referrals are made for services that VA is unable to provide.

Certain VA benefits including medical care require wartime service. Recognized wartime periods are shown in Table below.

VETERANS AFFAIRS RECOGNIZED WAR TIME PERIODS

- World War II: Dec. 7, 1941, through Dec. 31, 1946,
- Korean War: June 27, 1950, through Jan. 31, 1955,
- Vietnam War: Aug. 5, 1964 through May 7, 1975, (Feb. 28, 1961, for those who served "in country" before Aug. 5, 1964),
- Gulf War: Aug 2, 1990, through a date to be set by law or Presidential Proclamation.

IMPROVED PENSION / DEATH PENSION / AID & ATTENDANCE / HOUSEBOUND

While we will touch on several of the programs, the important programs to know for those interested in seeking assistance with payment for long term care costs are:

A. Improved Pension (for qualified veterans); and
B. Death Pension (for the surviving spouse of an otherwise qualified veteran).

It is not clear why they call it a pension program. The VA does not make payment to any health care provider like an insurance company would. They make the payment directly to the veteran or surviving spouse. Perhaps that is why it is called a pension. Unlike Medicaid which makes the payment to the facility, veteran's benefits through this program are payable to the individual.

GENERAL RULES FOR PENSION ELIGIBILITY

The rules for pension eligibility are as follows. The applicant must:

1. Be age 65 or older or, under 65 and totally and permanently disabled;

81

2. Have received other than a dishonorable discharge;
3. Served for 90 days or more, one day of which was during an active wartime operation. The applicant did not have to be in a combat zone, he or she need only have been in active service during an active wartime operation. See the Table for dates.
4. Have a financial need for the additional funds to pay for his or her care (or that of his or her spouse); and
5. Have assets less than a certain amount, typically $80,000 for a married couple (not counting their home nor vehicle). The asset amount must be such that, given the life expectancy of the veteran, their income and costs of care, the veteran needs the assets to supplement the costs of care. The asset threshold allowance is made by the subjective determination of the caseworker reviewing the case for the VA.

Being Rated – Aid & Attendance / Housebound

Both the Improved Pension and the Death Pension have supplemental payment programs. One is called Housebound and the other is called Aid & Attendance. Generally speaking, a veteran or spouse will apply for Aid & Attendance benefits if the individual is living in a personal care home or assisted living facility. If they are living at home, housebound might be a supplemental payment they will receive. Housebound pays a smaller amount than Aid & Attendance. If you are eligible for a supplemental payment, you are said to be "rated" for that supplemental program payment. A rating for "aid and attendance" or "housebound" allows VA to pay additional benefits beyond the regular Pension benefit ceiling in order to help cover the additional costs associated with added disabilities. A veteran service representative who has been trained to recognize from medical reports and interviews whether the veteran or his surviving spouse needs the additional care determines a rating for these allowances.

Determinations of a need for aid and attendance or housebound benefits may be based on medical reports and findings by private physicians or from hospital facilities. Authorization of aid and attendance benefits without a rating decision is automatic if evidence establishes the claimant is a patient in a nursing home. Aid and attendance is also automatic if the claimant is blind or nearly blind or having severe visual problems.

The U.S. Code of Federal Regulations provides the following criteria used to determine the need for aid and attendance:

- Inability of claimant to dress or undress himself (herself), or to keep himself (herself) ordinarily clean and presentable;
- Frequent need of adjustment of any special prosthetic or orthopedic appliances, which by reason of the particular disability cannot be done without aid (this will not include the adjustment of appliances which normal persons would be unable to adjust without aid, such as supports, belts, lacing at the back, etc.);
- Inability of claimant to feed himself (herself) through loss of coordination of upper extremities or through extreme weakness;
- Inability to attend to the wants of nature;
- Or incapacity, physical or mental, which requires care or assistance on a regular basis to protect the claimant from

hazards or dangers incident to his or her daily environment.

Not all of the disabling conditions in the list above are required to exist before a favorable rating may be made. The personal functions, which the veteran is unable to perform, are considered in connection with his or her condition as a whole. It is only necessary that the evidence establish that the veteran is so helpless as to need "regular" (scheduled and ongoing) aid and attendance from another person. There is no requirement that there be a 24-hour need.

"Bedridden" is a definition that allows a rating for aid and attendance by itself. "Bedridden" is a condition which requires that the claimant remain in bed. A person who has voluntarily taken to bed or who has been told by the doctor to remain in bed will not necessarily receive the favorable rating for aid and attendance. There must be an actual need for personal assistance from others.

Housebound means "permanently housebound by reason of disability or disabilities." This requirement is met when the veteran or his or her widow is substantially confined to his or her dwelling and the immediate premises or, if institutionalized, to the ward or clinical area, and it is reasonably certain that the disability or disabilities and resultant confinement will continue throughout his or her lifetime.

A person who cannot leave his immediate premises unless under the supervision of another person is considered housebound. This might include the inability to drive because of the disability.

A housebound rating does not mean a person needs to be confined to a personal residence. It can apply to any place where the person is living whether in a facility or in the home of someone else.

In order to receive one of these ratings the claimant must check the "Yes" box on VA Form 21-526 (claim for a living veteran) or VA Form 21-534 (claim for death Pension from a surviving spouse) that states: "Are you claiming a special monthly Pension because you need the regular assistance of another person, are blind, nearly blind, or having severe visual problems, or are housebound?" Failure to check this box may result in no rating and in some cases a denial of the claim as well as a loss of the rating allowance.

Medical evidence for a rating for "aid and attendance" or "housebound" for living arrangements other than a nursing home should be submitted with the application to avoid a delay in the approval process. Waiting for the regional office to order medical records is a time-consuming process, mainly because doctor's offices don't respond quickly to these kinds of requests.

It is highly recommended that a report be completed by the physician, and obtained by the family prior to submission of the claim. This report is then included with the initial application. Ratings are requested by checking the appropriate box for aid and attendance or housebound on VA Form 21-526 or VA Form 21-534.

Finally, a little understood provision exists that if a qualified veteran or surviving spouse gets at least $1.00 or more of benefits from the Aid & Attendance or housebound programs, that person is entitled to obtain their prescription drugs from the VA.

UNDERSTANDING
THE PENSION PAYMENT

First of all, in order to receive Aid & Attendance or Housebound benefits, the individual must first be eligible for a Pension, Improved or Death (Veteran or surviving spouse). If the person is not eligible for a pension, he or she is not eligible for either of the two supplemental payments. Thus you need to understand Pension first. The difficulty is in understanding the financial aspects. Begin by determining your monthly gross income. Then determine the annual, unreimbursed medical expenses (UME) including the costs of caregivers, medical insurance, physician co-pays, cost of an assisted living facility, etc. Divide that annual cost by 12 to determine the monthly amount. From the UME subtract 5% of the monthly pension amount. Now, subtract the UME with the 5% deduction and subtract that number from your gross monthly income. That is your IVAP (Income for VA Purposes). If the number is zero or less, you will receive the full pension amount. If the number is greater than zero, you may receive the amount of the benefit minus the IVAP amount.

Example. Joan is the surviving spouse of a World War II veteran. She is eligible for benefits under the Aid & Attendance program. Joan receives $2,000 a month in gross income and has care and medical costs of $1,900 a month. Because she is a surviving spouse, Joan's monthly unreimbursed medical expenses must be reduced by 5% of the surviving spouse death pension amount ($36). Joan's monthly unreimbursed medical expenses, minus the 5% are then $1,864 ($1,900 - $36). If you then subtract that amount from Joan's gross income of $2,000, Joan's IVAP would be $136 ($2,000 - $1864). Since Joan is eligible for Aid & Attendance, her maximum benefit would be $978 ($1,149 the maximum surviving spouse Aid & Attendance benefit less her IVAP of $136).

To further understand the distinction between the two Pension and the two supplemental payments for those rated (Aid & Attendance and Housebound), consider this scenario. What if the veteran is in generally good health but the surviving spouse is in need of an assisted living facility? The spouse is not a veteran. The answer is, that because the veteran is not in need of the aid and attendance of another, neither Aid & Attendance nor Housebound are available. However Improved Pension is available and the vet and his spouse may be able to obtain those funds if they otherwise qualify.

Try thinking of it this way, Pension, improved and/or death, are to assist a qualified veteran or surviving spouse of a deceased veteran with financial assistance with their medical bills when the bills reach a certain threshold. If the veteran or surviving spouse have reached a point in their lives where they can no longer independently take care of themselves, and are in need of the aid and attendance of another human being to help take care of them, or are unable to independently leave their home without assistance of another, they may be eligible for additional funds from the supplemental payment programs, Aid & Attendance or Housebound, respectively.

INCOME REQUIREMENTS

The veteran's income for his or her household cannot be greater than the Maximum Allowable Pension Rate (See Table inset). However, the income must be adjusted formedical bills. Far too many people hear that their income cannot be greater than the MAPR, look to see that the MAPR in their case is, say $1,731 and give up because their income is greater than $1,731 per month. The term used for VA income is IVAP, Income for VA Purposes. IVAP is your household income minus certain Unreimbursed Medical Expenses (UME).

2015 MAXIMUM ALLOWABLE PENSION RATES (MAPR)

Single Veteran Pension Only	$1,072.00
Single Veteran HouseBound	$1,310.00
Single Veteran Aid Attendance	$1,788.00
Surviving Spouse Pension Only	$ 719.00
Surviving Spouse HouseBound	$ 879.00
Surviving Spouse Aid Attendance	$1,149.00
Married Veteran Pension Only	$1,404.00
Married Veteran HouseBound	$1,642.00
Married Veteran Aid Attendance	$2,120.00

Here is the best way to calculate your potential benefit using 2015 numbers.

A = Your Annual Gross Household Income.

B = Your Annual Unreimbursed Medical Expenses (UME) for the upcoming year.

C = Your Maximum Allowable Pension Rate (MAPR).

D = The MAPR 5% annual deduction ($816 for Married Vet, $624 for a Single Vet, $408 for an eligible Surviving Spouse).

E = B – D [Adjusted UME after deduction of 5% of MAPR].

F = A – E [Gross annual income minus Adjusted UME. This is your Income for VA Purposes (IVAP). If F is less than zero, enter a zero.]
G = C – F [This is Your Annual Benefit].

Another, perhaps faster way to calculate your potential benefit is to take your MAPR, subtract your income and add back the adjusted UME. The result is your benefit but only up to the MAPR.

If the adjusted income exceeds MAPR, there is no benefit. If adjusted income is less than the MAPR, the veteran receives a pension income that is equal to the difference between MAPR and the household income adjusted for unreimbursed medical expenses. The pension income is calculated, based on 12 months of future household income, but paid monthly.

ASSET RULES

There is also an asset test to qualify for pension. Any asset or investment that could be easily converted into income might disqualify the claimant. An asset ceiling of $80,000 is often cited in the media as being the test. The $80,000 has to do with VA internal filing requirements and is not an actual test. In reality, there is no dollar amount for the test and any level of assets could block the award. The asset test ultimately becomes a subjective decision made by the veterans' service representative, processing the application. A home, used as a residence, vehicles and difficult-to-sell property are generally excluded from the asset test.

UNDERSTANDING THE $80,000 LIMIT

The real test of an applicant's assets is whether or not the applicant has excessive assets. The VA has tables to determine an applicant's life expectancy. Given the age of the applicant and his or her life expectancy, the question becomes; "Will the applicant run out of money in his or her lifetime given the person's income and medical expenses?" In other words, how long will your assets last given the monthly drain of medical expenses?

If an applicant's assets are greater than the $80,000 threshold, this test will be applied. If the assets are less than this threshold, the test typically will not be conducted. You can calculate your own VA life expectancy and asset test estimator using our on line tools (See our website www.GoodLTC. com).

USING AN ATTORNEY

Far too many people try to do things on their own. They do not want to work with an elder law attorney and pay attorney's fees for the necessary planning and application review. This can often turn out to be penny wise and pound-foolish. Taking the time to work with an attorney can prevent many other issues that arise during the application process. By taking this step you will be assured to be in the best position possible to receive the benefit with the least amount of hassle, and in the shortest period of time.

Unfortunately, many people try to reduce their assets below the $80,000 threshold on their own. This is never a good idea. Gifting to qualify for VA benefits is a complicated strategy and if done without the advice of professionals, can have many negative complications. You should always discuss any large gift or asset transfer with an attorney or CPA to make sure that it does not have unintended tax and other negative consequences for you and your family in the future. While there currently is no penalty for gifting in order to receive VA benefits, there are harsh penalties assessed to gifts made in an effort to qualify for Medicaid. Do-it-yourself planning for VA may make you ineligible for Medicaid down the road. A qualified elder law attorney will help to highlight and address negative issues for you and put you in a position to maximize both benefits.

DOCUMENTATION REQUIREMENTS

The veteran must provide an original copy of discharge from service, typically a DD 214 discharge certificate. A photocopy is allowed if it is certified by a government agency recognized to do this. This could be the local courthouse. For a surviving spouse death benefit, a death certificate must be furnished as well. VA may request copies of other documents, but, generally, providing sufficient information on the claim form will satisfy the need for other documentation. If an applicant for pension is younger than 65, medical evidence of total disability must also be submitted. Total disability for 65 and older is not a requirement for death pension.

START DATE OF ELIGIBILITY

The effective date is generally the day VA receives an original application. If it takes months for the process of approval, it doesn't matter. The effective date still reverts to receipt of the original application.

WHEN DOES PAYMENT BEGIN?

Generally, payments start on the first day of the month following the month of the effective date. This means that if it took six months to get approval, at least five months of benefit will be paid retroactively. VA requires automatic deposit of awards in a checking or savings account.

DEATH DURING THE PENDENCY OF AN APPLICATION

If the veteran dies during the period of application and the application was not approved prior to the death, there may be accrued benefits. If the regional office had all of the information in its possession that would have led to an approval, then there is an accrued benefit payable. Otherwise there is none. The full benefit is available up to the month of death of the veteran and to a surviving spouse through an application on Form 21-534. This is the same form a surviving spouse uses for a death benefit claim for himself or herself. VA will award either an accrued benefit or death benefit to the surviving spouse whichever is larger. If there is no surviving spouse or dependent child, VA will pay the unreimbursed costs of last illness and burial to the person who paid those costs. A special claim must be submitted for these costs, not Form 21-534.

BENEFITS TAXATION

The pension benefit is not typically subject to federal income taxation. However, if the veteran is making payments to a caregiver, those payments are earned income and are subject to income taxation.

PENSION AND MEDICAID

What about a veteran in a nursing home on Medicaid? If a qualified veteran or surviving spouse is in a nursing home and is paying privately, they will receive VA benefits if otherwise qualified. However, once that veteran goes onto Medicaid, the payment amount drops from wherever it was to $90.00 per month.

ELIGIBILITY FOR
A FEDERAL VETERANS HOME

The Veterans Home is now called the Community Living Center. To be eligible for nursing home care, you must be enrolled in or eligible for the VA health care system. Nursing home care is available for veterans rated 70 percent service-connected or greater and veterans who need nursing home care for their service-connected disabilities.

STATE NURSING HOMES FOR VETERANS

Back in the times of the Civil War, many states built and developed homes for disabled and homeless veterans. While the VA certifies and recognizes these homes, the VA does not run them. The state government runs them. Every state has its own set of rules. Pennsylvania's rules require the applicant be; 1) an honorably discharged veteran, spouse of an honorably discharged veteran, or surviving spouse of an honorably discharged veteran; 2) a bona fide resident of Pennsylvania whose home of record upon entry into the armed forces was Pennsylvania; 3) required to make monthly payments against the maintenance fee liability in accordance with his ability to pay; and 4) admission shall be on a first-come, first-served basis.

The following individuals are not eligible. 1) An applicant who requires mental health care or custody; 2) an applicant whose behavior creates a reasonable threat to the health, safety and welfare of other residents, even when the applicant is under medications to control this behavior; 3) an applicant whose level of care or treatment is not available in the state home; 4) an applicant with a contagious disease; and 5) an applicant convicted of a felony unless the person has shown good character and behavior and has no convictions of crimes or offenses for at least five years subsequent to incarceration.

Beware! Just as Medicaid has an estate recovery program, so do the State Veterans homes, at least in Pennsylvania. Recently there has been a good deal of news on the shock the families of deceased veterans upon learning that the state would seek to recover the costs expended on individuals whom they cared for in state veterans homes. As with the remainder of all areas covered in this book, it is imperative that you have an experienced elder law attorney advising you on the dangers of any particular program.

MEDAL OF HONOR PENSION

VA administers pensions to recipients of the Medal of Honor. The monthly pension amount is currently $1,237.00.

OTHER VETERAN PROGRAMS

Requirements for benefits have changed from time to time. Some benefits today do not require a service-related injury, although they may require copayments for veterans whose family income and assets exceed the annual limit for no-cost service. These and other benefits may apply:

- Respite care to relieve family caregivers of veterans with dementia.
- Medical care for eligible veterans who served during war times.

- Disability compensation for veterans with service-related injuries.
- Burial benefits for eligible veterans.

1. RESPITE CARE

VA medical centers often provide respite care for eligible Alzheimer's or related dementia veterans being cared for by a caregiver in the community. Up to 14 days of custodial care may be provided as often as once every six months. Check with the VA Medical Center. A Facility Locator is found on the Veterans Administration website, www.va.gov.

2. MEDICAL CARE

To receive health care, veterans generally must be enrolled with the VA. A veteran may apply for enrollment at any time. Veterans do not have to be enrolled if they: (1) have a service-connected disability of 50% or more; (2) want care for disability, which the military determined was incurred or aggravated in the line of duty, but which VA has not yet rated, during the 12 month period following discharge: or (3) want care for a service-connected disability only.

Veterans will be enrolled to the extent congressional appropriations allow. If appropriations are limited, enrollment will occur based on the following priorities:

- Veterans with service-connected conditions rated 50% or more disabled.
- Veterans with service-connected conditions rated 30 or 40% disabled.
- Veterans who are former POWs or were awarded a Purple Heart, veterans with disabilities rated 10 and 20%,

and veterans awarded special eligibility for disabilities incurred in treatment.

- Veterans who are receiving aid and attendance or house-bound benefits and veterans who have been determined by VA to be catastrophically disabled.
- Nonservice-connected veterans and service-connected veterans rated zero percent, noncompensable disabled, who are determined to be unable to defray the expenses of needed care.
- Nonservice-connected veterans and noncompensable zero percent service-connected veterans who agree to pay copayments.

The Veterans' Millennium Health Care and Benefits Act of 1999 authorized VA to expand long-term care services and to reimburse emergency treatment expenses for certain enrolled veterans.

Veterans who want to enroll in priority group 5 based on their inability to defray the cost of their care must provide VA with information on their annual income and net worth to determine whether they are below the "means test" threshold or agree to copayment requirements. The threshold is adjusted annually and announced in January. In making the assessment, the veteran's household income is considered.

The "means test" eligibility assessment includes income such as Social Security, U.S. Civil Service retirement, U.S. Railroad retirement, military retirement, unemployment insurance, any other retirement income, total wages from all employers, interest and dividends, workers' compensation, black lung benefits and any other gross income for the calendar year prior to application for care. Also considered are assets such as the market value of stocks, bonds, notes, individual retirement accounts, bank deposits, savings accounts and cash. The patient may fill out VA form 10-10EZ at the time application for enrollment is made. VA may compare income information provided by the veteran with information obtained from the Social Security Administration and the Internal Revenue Service.

After a veteran completes a financial assessment that determines the veteran's income and assets are above the "means test" threshold, the veteran must agree to pay copayments to be eligible for VA care. VA holds older patients whose income is determined to be above the "means test" threshold responsible for the Medicare deductible for the first 90 days of care during any 365-day period. For each additional 90 days of hospital care, the patient is charged one-half the Medicare deductible. For each additional 90 days of nursing-home care, the patient is again charged the full Medicare deductible. In addition to these charges, the patient is charged copays for hospital care and VA nursing-home care.

VA is authorized to submit claims to health insurance carriers for recovery of VA's reasonable charges in providing medical care to nonservice-connected veterans and to service-connected veterans for nonservice-connected conditions.

All veterans applying for VA medical care will be asked to provide information on their health insurance coverage, including coverage provided under policies of their spouses. Although veterans are not responsible for paying any remaining balance of VA's insurance claim that is not paid or covered by their health insurance, veterans whose income is above the "means test" threshold are responsible for the VA's copayments required by federal law. However, when VA receives payment from the veteran's health insurance company or the care furnished, VA credits that recovery toward the amount of the veteran's copayment obligation.

3. DISABILITY COMPENSATION

VA disability compensation is a monetary benefit paid to veterans who are disabled by injury or disease incurred and aggravated during active military service. The service of the veteran must have been terminated through separation or discharge under conditions that were other than dishonorable. Disability compensation varies with the degree of disability and the number of dependents. It is paid monthly. The benefits are not subject to federal and state income tax. The payment of military retirement pay, a disability severance pay and separation incentive payment affects the amount of VA compensation paid.

Former prisoners of war who were incarcerated for at least 30 days are presumed to be eligible for disability compensation if they become at least 10 percent disabled from diseases associated with POWs. These presumptive diseases are avitaminosis, beriberi, heart disease and ischemic heart disease where the prisoner of war experienced localized edema during captivity, chronic dysentery, helminthiasis. Also included are malnutrition including optic atrophy, pellagra and other nutritional deficiencies, psychosis, anxiety states and dysthymic disorder or depressive neurosis, post traumatic osteoarthritis, irritable bowel syndrome, peptic ulcer, and arthritis, neuropathy and skin cancer at the site of the old injury.

4. BURIAL BENEFITS

Five burial benefits are available for veterans who were honorably discharged:

1. United States flag is provided at no cost to drape the casket or accompany the urn of a deceased veteran.
2. Families of veterans on VA Disability or Pension at the time of death may receive a burial and funeral allowance.
3. Veterans and dependents may be buried in National Cemeteries.
4. A Presidential Memorial Certificate expressing the country's thanks is available for families of deceased veterans.
5. Upright stones and flat grave markers are available for the veteran regardless of whether interment is in a VA or private cemetery. Spouses and dependents may qualify if burial is in a National Cemetery.

MEDICAID

13

For many or you, the topic of interest in this book is this chapter. Medicaid for long term care is the largest payer in the country without a close second. Medicaid pays for peoples' care because they cannot afford the high costs of nursing home care. We've seen people go through their life savings on the costs of long-term care. One couple's family came to see us, informing us that the parent had spent over $1 million on nursing home care costs over the past 10 years. Few people can afford $8,000 plus per month. Medicaid eligibility is also a very dangerous field for anyone to try to manage without expert advice.

Medicaid law is one of the most complicated areas of law in this country. Medicaid law has been described by numerous judges throughout the land as an incomprehensible maze. Another referred to it as a *Serbonian Bog* for the uninitiated. Serbonian Bog refers to the lake of Serbonis in Egypt. Because sand blew onto it, the Serbonian Bog had a deceptive appearance of being solid land, but was a bog that trapped people from which they could not escape. Another judge stated that Medicaid law is one of the "most completely impenetrable texts within human experience" and "dense reading of the most tortuous kind."

Medicaid is the central area of law in which Elder Law attorneys specialize. If you are in California, Medicaid is called Medi-Cal. Pennsylvania calls it Medical Assistance or MA (em-ay). Massachusetts calls it MassHealth, Tennessee has TennCare and Maine has MaineCare. The federal name is Medicaid and that is what I will refer to it as throughout this book. Medicaid is a massive area of the law that covers so many different areas and programs it would take a multi-volume set of books to attempt to describe it. While there are many programs run by the each state's Medicaid department, in this book we will be dealing only with the long term care aspects and programs of Medicaid.

In law school we are taught that there is no one right answer to most legal questions. That is a difficult mindset to attain. Medicaid takes that precept and multiplies it one hundred fold. Why is Medicaid so complicated? Well to begin with, it is a federal law or program. It has federal statutes and federal regulations. In addition, each state, in order to participate in Medicaid must formulate its own plan on how each will provide Medicaid benefits to each state's respective citizens. Therefore, there are state statutes and regulations as well. In addition, there is practice and custom in each state, even each county. They all provide Medicaid benefits in their own way. I can tell you that there are drastically different rules in the western half of Pennsylvania than there are in the eastern half.

Earlier in this book I referred to the Medicaid waiver programs, numerous programs in every state. The waiver programs are programs where the state wishes to use Medicaid dollars for a program that does not quite comport with standard Medicaid law so they seek a waiver of the requirement. Talk about complicated!

You must hire a capable, experienced elder law attorney to assist you if you or a loved one is applying for Medicaid for long term care. This book is not intended to be a replacement for a lawyer. It is designed to help you to understand what is going on so that you can try to better understand the system. When I explain the Medicaid laws to my clients, 100% of them have been confused. Our clients have included people of all education levels and all walks of life. Our clients have even included lawyers and judges. I tell them at the onset that they will be confused. Jokingly I state, "If you are confused, then you understand. But if you think you understand, then you are confused!" It takes a while to understand the system, even years. There is a reason why every general practitioner lawyer does not work in elder law. Medicaid is too confusing and the risks are too great.

That brings me to another key point. Because it is so confusing, you cannot expect that the caseworker who is working on your Medicaid application will know all of the laws. Being a caseworker is a very difficult and stressful job. People come and go in this position. You must not expect them to; a) know all of the intricacies of the law or, b) to properly apply the law to your case. Most of them do their best. There is simply too much to know and you cannot pick it up and understand it quickly. If you have an elder law attorney on your side, you will have an individual who knows the law better than anyone else including the caseworkers. A lawyer never states, "That's not what I was told." Saying that's not what I was told is not legal authority. Statutes, regulations and precedent are the law and an attorney can point right to it to persuade the caseworker or judge if your case is on appeal. You may also experience what your state's Medicaid agency refers to as policy. They often refer to policy as a sort of legal authority in their application of Medicaid. Let me state quite clearly that "policy" is not law. I have seen many of our state's policies attempted to be applied in ways that are completely contradictory to the mandates of the law. Watch out for policy.

With all of those warnings placed before you, let's discuss Medicaid in further detail. Medicaid is a federal program that is administered by the states. It came about at the same time Medicare did, 1965. The federal government agency responsible for Medicaid is called CMS, the Centers for Medicare and Medicaid Services. It used to be called the Health Care Financing Administration (HCFA). Every state is required to provide and maintain a plan called the State Plan that describes how they will utilize Medicaid dollars. You see, much of the money that is used for Medicaid services is provided by the federal government. The state does provide some of its own but a large amount is federal.

It is also important to note that Medicaid is the largest part of most every state's budget. Because it is so large and uses so much of each state's budget, the states have very tight controls on how the money is paid out.

Remember that your state might do things a little differently than I show here. For the most part I am going to limit this topic to federal law and my examples will be from a Pennsylvania law perspective. Every state has its own way of working with the Medicaid program. Here are a couple of examples. In Florida, if an applicant's income is over a certain amount, the income must go into a trust fund called a Miller Trust. In Pennsylvania, Medicaid is not available to pay for care in an assisted living facility. Medicaid will pay for care in an assisted living facility for Ohio residents. Here is a quiz question for you. I, a citizen of Florida in a nursing home, come to Pennsylvania to be cared for by my sister who lives in Pennsylvania. If otherwise eligible, am I A) Covered by Florida Medicaid, B) Covered by Pennsylvania Medicaid, C) Not Covered at all or D) Covered by my choice. The correct answer is B. Payment for care in a Pennsylvania nursing home will be covered by Pennsylvania's medical assistance program administered by Pennsylvania's Department of Human Services (formerly Department of Public Welfare).

THE SINGLE VS. MARRIED APPLICANT

There are different sets of rules for single people versus married couples. In 1988 Congress passed a law called MCCA (pronounced Mecca), the Medicare Catastrophic Coverage Act. Do not be confused by the term Medicare. Everyone confuses the two. Medicare and Medicaid are two completely different programs. There are huge differences between them. Even though it says Medicare in the law's title, the portion we are discussing involves Medicaid, NOT Medicare. MCCA changed Medicaid drastically. Medicaid was and is a health insurance safety net for the poor. It was and is a welfare program. However MCCA changed all of that and made it an insurance program to cover long term care expenses for middle class married couples. Imagine if you will, a married couple where one requires nursing home care and all of the income of the ill spouse has to go to the nursing home and they are permitted to have assets of no more than $2,000.00. People were literally eating dog food to survive. MCCA came about to change that and has a complex set of rules that we will endeavor to explain to you in this chapter. The goal of MCCA was to make certain that the healthier spouse, termed the *Community Spouse*, had enough assets to survive on and enough income to pay the monthly bills.

As we go through this chapter, we will explain each set of rules as they apply to a single applicant for Medicaid and the set of rules that apply to a married couple.

THE FIVE AREAS TO UNDERSTAND

It is easier to understand Medicaid by breaking it down into five areas of rules. They are:
1. Medical Eligibility;
2. Rules regarding Income;
3. Rules regarding Assets;
4. Gifting Rules; and
5. Estate Recovery.

1. MEDICAL ELIGIBILITY

One cannot simply move into a nursing home (or be placed there) unless that person meets the medical eligibility requirements. The person must be unable to care for him or herself and require assistance with the Activities of Daily Living or ongoing supervision. A rule of thumb is that the person is unable to independently perform two or more of the ADLs. There are safeguards to assure that the person needs that level of care. In Pennsylvania, Medicaid is administered by the State

Department of Public Welfare but medical eligibility is determined by each county's Area Agency on Aging. An individual assessment is performed by the county and the county must make a determination that the person requires long term care in a nursing home. It used to be called an OPTIONS assessment. It is now termed LOCA, Level of Care Assessment. A nursing home determination can be either short term (six months or less) or long term (more than six months).

INCOME OR ASSET?

While what I am about to state may seem obvious to some people, it is not to others. There is a significant distinction between assets and income. If you get a check every month from social security, from your pension fund, from an annuity, or from your employment, that is income. Your income gets added to your assets.

Your assets are bank accounts, investment accounts, life insurance policies, vehicles, real estate, etc. Many people do not understand the difference but they are significant if you are to understand how Medicaid operates.

REMEMBER THIS

Every state does things a little bit differently. Many counties within each state do things a little bit differently. The rules are always changing.

2. RULES REGARDING INCOME
INCOME FOR A SINGLE PERSON

For a single individual, the rules for income are quite simple, the monthly income checks are split three ways. The nursing home resident is permitted to keep a certain amount called the personal needs allowance. In Pennsylvania that amount is $45 per month. They are also permitted (even required) to continue to make payments for their monthly health insurance including a prescription drug plan if they have one. The balance is paid to the nursing home. You continue to maintain your Medicare or health insurance. If the person becomes hospitalized, that insurance pays the bill, not Medicaid. Medicaid will only pay what is not paid by another source. Medicaid is called the "Payer of Last Resort."

INCOME FOR A MARRIED COUPLE

Federal law provides protections for the income needs of the Community Spouse called the monthly maintenance needs allowance (MMNA). Federal law prescribes that the MMNA should equal at least 150% of the federal poverty level for a couple ($1,992) per month in 2015 - 2016 and be adjusted every July by the general rate of inflation. States have the option to use a higher minimum level -- $2,980 per month. Many states use this higher figure. Thirty-five did so at last count.

It works this way in Pennsylvania; you begin with the minimum amount. An analysis of the Community Spouse's shelter costs is determined on a monthly basis. Shelter costs are mortgage payments, real estate tax payments, homeowner insurance payments, rent payments, condominium fees, and utilities. If these monthly, prorated bills are greater than an amount called the shelter standard, the additional amount, the amount in excess of the shelter standard, is added onto the minimum monthly needs allowance ($1,992 in first half of 2016) and that is the amount of income the Community Spouse may have. Now, if the Community Spouse's current income is greater than that calculated amount, the

Community Spouse simply keeps all of his or her income. If it is less, the Community Spouse may be entitled to a portion of income from the nursing home spouse to bring the income level up to the MMNA. On occasion, the combined income of the Community Spouse and the nursing home spouse is not enough to bring the Community Spouse up to the MMNA amount. In those circumstances, in Pennsylvania, a calculation is made which will permit the Community Spouse to keep additional assets from the spend-down. Understand how important it is for you to see your elder law attorney as soon as possible. If you learn later on that you were entitled to keep additional assets and spent them on the nursing home instead, you will not be getting a refund from anyone. You need to be proactive and act earlier rather than later. Here again, timing comes into play.

There is a maximum amount allowed for income. This can be confusing. The Community Spouse has no maximum income as long as the income is his or hers. But, there is a maximum that can be calculated and taken from the nursing home spouse's income. This is called the maximum MMNA. In 2015-2016, that amount is $2,980.50. This issue arises when the Community Spouse has a large mortgage payment or high rent (from an assisted living facility). Often the MMNA will be greater than the maximum, especially when the Community Spouse is in an assisted living facility. When your MMNA is calculated at greater than the maximum MMNA, you must seek court approval for the larger amount. This will be granted in most cases where the need is clear and obvious such as when the Community Spouse is in an assisted living facility. *Court* does not mean court with an older man or woman in a black robe. Court here is an administrative judge and usually takes place over the telephone.

NAME ON THE CHECK RULE

In determining what is his income and what is her income, we use the "name on the check." This includes pension benefits, social security benefits, IRA payouts in some states, or other income paid only to the account holder, and accessible by the spouse only if deposited in a joint account. Income the couple receives jointly is divided in half. The nursing home spouse owns half and the Community Spouse owns half. Otherwise, whoever's name is on the check receives that income.

In Pennsylvania, a married nursing home resident will have his or her income split 4 ways; $45 for his or her personal needs allowance, payment of his or her monthly health insurance premiums, the amount needed by the Community Spouse to bring the Community Spouse's income up to the MMNA, and the balance goes to the nursing home. Medicaid pays on top of that to make up the shortfall based upon the legal coverage amount provided by Medicaid in their agreement with the nursing home for the level of care required.

For example. John is in a nursing home. He receives $1,200 in social security and $600 from a pension. Mary is the Community Spouse and she has $600 a month in social security income. Her MMNA was calculated at $2,000. Mary keeps her income and can take $1,400 from John. John then pays $150 for his health insurance premium, keeps $45, pays $1,400 to Mary, and pays the difference $205 to the nursing home. If Mary does not receive any of John's pension when he dies, or even one-half, there is a possible need for a DRA annuity here. Do you see that?

HOME MAINTENANCE ALLOWANCE

Imagine, if you will, someone of very limited means, who is able to qualify for Medicaid payment very quickly because of his or her assets and income. What if that person owns a home? What if that person will be returning to that home and is only in the nursing home temporarily? If Medicaid requires that person to pay all of his or her income to the nursing home, he or she will be unable to pay for property taxes, insurance, utilities and maintenance on the home. That issue has been considered and addressed. If the nursing home resident is predicted to be short term, typically six months or less, the state Medicaid agency will permit the resident to retain an amount for these home bills. In the year 2015, Pennsylvania's allowance is $755.10. Different states may apply this law and the corresponding amount differently.

THE MODIFIED HURLY

This can be a bit complicated. What if, in the above example, the husband Ned does not have $1,370.10 to give his wife? What if his available income is only $1,000? Where does Cheryl make up that $370.10 monthly difference? In Pennsylvania this is now called a PAR (Protect Additional Resources) proceeding. It was formerly called a Hurly Appeal named after a lawsuit from many years ago. A PAR proceeding is when the income of both spouses is not sufficient to bring the Community Spouse up to his or her MMNA. In our example, $370.10. Using the modified Hurly, the Community spouse must ascertain his or her life expectancy and find out what it would cost him or her to purchase an annuity that would pay, Cheryl in this case $370.00 per month for the remainder of her life expectancy. Life expectancy can be determined by a set of tables published by the State. Let's say that for Cheryl's life expectancy, an annuity would cost her $35,000. In addition to her normal CSRA, Cheryl may keep an additional $35,000 from her spend down. Cheryl does not have to purchase an annuity. The annuity price is simply a tool to determine how much she can keep.

What most often goes wrong with a PAR proceeding is that the family does not realize they are eligible for this until after they've already spent down their money. No one gives refunds so you have basically lost this important option. A good elder law attorney would or should do an estimate of your financial position early on, before you've spent down.

3. RULES REGARDING ASSETS

The rules regarding what assets a Medicaid recipient for long-term care is allowed to keep vary from state to state. You need to hire an elder law attorney to help you know the rules for your state. Generally speaking, a single Medicaid applicant is permitted to have either $2,400 or $8,000 in Pennsylvania depending on his or her income level. His or her spouse may keep much more.

MEDICAID ELIGIBILITY AND THE SSI RULES

There is a federal social security program called Supplemental Security Income (SSI). SSI is a welfare program that pays a certain amountto individuals who are unable to work due to a physical or mental impairment that prevents them from sub-stantial gainful employment. Often times, a person born with a disability will at some point in their lifetime receive SSI. In many (not all) states, a person who receives SSI receives Medicaid automatically. Just so you are aware, there are two basic forms of social security disability payments. The first is SSI, the second is SSD. The basic distinctions are these; social security disability (SSD) is for people who worked and paid into the social security and Medicare systems. They receive payments, the amount of which is based upon their work history. There are no asset rules or limitations to receive SSD. In addition, the person on SSD usually can apply for Medicare after two years on SSD. A person does not receive Medicaid when on SSD while they will probably receive Medicaid if on SSI (depending upon whether their state is deemed an "SSI State").

Why the background on SSI? Because the rules for SSI eligibility are the basis for the federal rules for Medicaid eligibility. I've said it over and over again, but these rules vary and it is critical that you speak with an elder law attorney to help you. For a single applicant, typically a person is permitted to have $2,000.00 in assets. Pennsylvania allows a person to have either $2,400 or $8,000 depending upon their income. How do you know what assets are included? Your House? Car? Life Insurance? The below listed assets are not countable. In other words they do not form part of the $2,400/$8,000 one is permitted to retain:

Non-Countable Assets
- Your home (provided that its equity value is less than $552,000);
- $2,400.00 or $8,000;
- One automobile;
- Personal property (jewelry, etc.);
- Home furnishings;
- Life Insurance, provided that the total face value is not greater than $1,500 regardless of cash value;
- Group or Term Life Insurance;

- Irrevocable burial reserves (aka prepaid funerals);
- Burial plots;
- A Business where someone relies on it for self-support.
- In Pennsylvania but not in all states, the IRA, 401K or employer sponsored retirement plan of the Community (non-nursing home) Spouse is not countable.

Now that you know what is non-countable, I can tell you that countable is everything else. Countable assets are primarily cash, stocks, bonds, mutual funds, annuities, all bank accounts, real estate that is not your home, any other motor vehicle, life insurance cash value, etc.

Joint Accounts

If the applicant has a joint account, say a checking account and that account is titled in the name of the applicant and another person and it has $10,000.00, how much of that is considered countable? The answer is; $10,000.00, the whole amount. Now if it can be proven that the other owner of the account contributed money to the account and can do so by clear documentary evidence, the Medicaid agency will deem that portion to be considered as owned by the other person (not the applicant) rendering it non-countable. The presumption is that the money belongs to the applicant and can be used for his or her care.

Married Couple Accounts

Almost every married couple that I've dealt with has approached us with "this is in my name and that is in her name" or something to that effect. As with joint accounts held with another person, the same applies to married couples. It does not matter if an account is in his name or her name or joint names. When it comes to determining countable assets for a married couple, what is in his name counts, what is in her name counts and what is in joint names counts, 100%. For married couples, look at the forest, not the trees. In the next section I will be discussing countable assets for a married couple and how that amount is determined. Don't look at individual accounts, look at everything and add it up no matter which spouse's name is on that account or investment. Look at that big picture in terms of the amount of everything added together. With married couples everything is valued as of the snapshot date. The snapshot date is the date your spouse entered the nursing home. Everything gets valued as of that day. The lump sum of everything, valued as of that day, is the amount that determines how much the non nursing home spouse (called the Community Spouse) can keep. The couple will go through a spend-down process. When that process is completed, the Community Spouse will have a protected share. The protected share is an amount, not individual assets. Frankly, if the Community Spouse's protected share is determined to be $100,000, it can be in any form the Community Spouse wishes. It can be in bank accounts, investment accounts, life insurance, whatever he or she wishes.

DETERMINING THE PROTECTED SHARE - *CSRA*

CSRA (pronounced is siz-ra), means Community Spouse Resource Allowance, the amount of assets the Community Spouse may keep to get Medicaid payment for his or her spouse's nursing home care. For married couples, as stated in the previous section, a snapshot of the assets of the couple and their countable assets is taken as of the date the spouse went into the nursing home. If it is a Medicaid application for home care or community-based waiver services, the snapshot is the date of application or the date the assessment is completed. Speak with an elder law attorney about how your state and locale manages that process.

The countable assets are valued as of the close of business that snapshot day and valued. That value is then divided in two. The Community Spouse may retain one-half of their countable assets in addition to the vehicle, home, and other non-countable assets. The nursing home spouse may retain the amount allowed for a single person, typically $2,400.00 / $8,000.00. There is a cap and a floor on what may be retained by the Community Spouse. This amount changes each January. In 2016, the cap or maximum amount the Community Spouse can retain of the countable assets is $119,220.00. The floor is $23,844.00. This is another area that varies from state to state.

For example, if the married couple has $100,000 in countable assets, the Community Spouse can retain one-half or $50,000, the nursing home spouse can retain $2,400 and the couple has a spend-down of $47,600. If the married couple has $40,000 in countable assets, the Community Spouse can retain $23,844, the nursing home spouse retains $8,000 and they have a spend-down of $8,156.00. If the couple has $300,000 in countable assets, the Community Spouse can retain $119,220.00, the nursing home spouse retains $2,400 and they have a spend-down of $178,380.00.

IS DIVORCE AN ALTERNATIVE?
What if the Community Spouse decides, rather than spend my life savings on my spouse's care, I divorce him/her? I'm sure that has occurred, many times. As with everything else in this field, I would suppose that there are zealous caseworkers who view

an attempt to divorce as a ploy to obtain Medicaid wrongly. Others may not. Nonetheless, divorce often involves equitable distribution of property as well as alimony. I don't know that divorce is going to have the effect many people envision.

WHAT ABOUT OUR PRENUPTIAL AGREEMENT?

Another problem area is prenuptial agreements (called pre-nups). A prenup is a contract signed by a husband and wife, either before they get married, or after being married. Both husband and wife agree to keep all of their assets separate and waive any interest in the other's estate when the other dies. Although other states or counties may differ, in our area prenups are not valid reasons to seek Medicaid benefits instead of supporting your spouse with your own funds. This is an extremely problematic area with or without prenups. Consider the problems that may develop between the families of people in a second (or third or more!) marriage when one spouse is in a nursing home and the other is at home. Spend down of the ailing spouse's assets seems just and proper. But what if that spouse brought more into the marriage? What if the nursing home spouse brought all or most all of the assets into the marriage and then gets ill and enters a nursing home? What occurs when he or she dies? Who gets the assets? The prenuptial agreement may state that the assets go to his or her family. But in order to get Medicaid, the surviving spouse had to transfer these assets to his or her name as the Community Spouse. Perhaps you can envision what some of these problems may become. See your elder law attorney for guidance.

SPOUSAL REFUSAL

There is federal law that essentially states that a state should provide Medicaid benefits to a married applicant if his or her spouse refuses to support him/her and the applicant spouse assigns the rights to support over to the state. This is a very difficult statute to apply and utilize. The state caseworkers are typically unaware of this statute and simply deny the application. You will need to review this statute with your elder law attorney.

TIME TO RETITLE

Since the nursing home spouse may only have $2,400 in his or her name, that means that the couple must now retitle assets. The nursing home spouse may only have $2,400 worth of assets. Everything except for that $2,400 must be in the name of the Community Spouse and not in the name of the nursing home spouse. Be careful here that you do not cause yourself more problems. The nursing home spouse undoubtedly has a bank account where his or her social security and other checks are deposited. If you remove his or her name and change accounts, you want to make certain that all automatic deposits are changed ahead of time.

WHAT IF THE COMMUNITY SPOUSE DIES FIRST?

This might be the most important section you can read in this book. What if the Community Spouse dies? What if the Will of the Community Spouse says everything goes to my spouse? What if the home is titled in joint names? The answer, at least in Pennsylvania if not the rest of the other states, is that the Medicaid recipient is now a single individual and may have no more in assets than any other single individual. If that is $2,000 then the Medicaid recipient will lose their benefits and the entire amount will be spent down on the nursing home. If that occurs, the life savings the couple worked so hard to save may be gone in its entirety, including the family home.

An elder law attorney can help greatly in this area. The possibility that the Community Spouse may die first must be reviewed and actions taken to minimize loss if that is the desire of the Community Spouse. Often times an elder law attorney will draft a Will for the Community Spouse that disinherits the nursing home spouse at least in part. That is permissible but most states have a law called the Elective Share law, which essentially provides that you cannot disinherit your spouse. In many states the spouse may take what they get under the Will (nothing if disinherited) or take 30% - 33% of everything. Because Medicaid law says that if there is money you can get, you must go out and get it and use it, the Community Spouse must use their election and take the elective share portion. Typically we will do that and simply pay that portion of the money (one third in Pennsylvania) over to the State of Pennsylvania and ask that they maintain the nursing home spouse on Medicaid. Very real and serious problems can develop if there is a prenuptial agreement between the spouses and the Medicaid agency is demanding the elective share be exercised. There is also an opportunity when that occurs. In many states the elective share may be waived. A prenuptial agreement usually contains a waiver. Thus, the surviving, Medicaid receiving, surviving spouse should be entitled to nothing. This can get complicated: see a qualified elder law attorney for help in this (and all other) areas.

What if the nursing home spouse refuses to take the elective share? Well the Medicaid agency can call that a gift and inflict a non-payment of benefits for a period of time based upon the value of the elective share. There is a federal statute that addresses what we elder law attorneys call spousal refusal (See above).

Cover all your bases. You should speak with your attorney and have a new Will drafted for the Community Spouse, title the house into the name of the Community Spouse alone, and change all beneficiary designations on IRAs, insurance policies and all other investments. Your attorney may also recommend a special needs trust. He or she will be of invaluable help. This is one of the many areas in elder law where you can get taken by surprise and lose everything.

Also, just to clear up one last item, I do not know of anyone having their home taken. People often say, "They'll take your home, they'll take all of your money, etc." While that may be the effect that is not what happens (although it used to years ago). Medicaid is a benefit for which one applies. There are rules for eligibility. If you meet the rules, you are eligible. If you do not, you may be forced to part with savings and assets to attain eligibility.

Pennsylvania's annual nursing home bill, on average, is over $105,000. Few can afford that for very long and you have no other choice but to sell your assets and pay your way until eligible for Medicaid.

Let me add one other note. While I stated that I have never seen the state or nursing home ever take someone's assets, that's not to say that it has never happened. In fact I would bet that it has happened many times. The difference is that it should not have happened. But if you go into a situation unprepared, inexperienced and without any solid knowledge of the rules of the game, you will likely lose. In that situation, the rules are whatever the other side, the State caseworker or nursing home personnel, say they are. These people are often told what the rules are by their supervisors and they apply them that way. Often times they are wrong and if you fight them with an elder law attorney at your side, you can at least be assured that you will have the rules applied to you properly.

SPEND DOWN

Spend down is one of the most important areas where an elder law attorney can help you. Far too often people believe that they must spend their money on the nursing home only. That is not the case. You absolutely need the help and guidance of an experienced elder law attorney in this area. Do not do this alone. Nor does it make sense for you to do it alone. The number one spend down item that is allowed is an attorney. You're not saving anything by doing it on your own. More clients than I can count have told me in the end that they did not fully comprehend that. Understand it. As long as you have spend down, you're not saving anything by doing things on your own. Also, of critical importance is **when** you spend your money (See below).

A good elder law attorney will look at your circumstances and help you spend your spend down money on the things you need. Some of those items include:
- Paying off mortgages and bills;
- Paying your tax bill;
- Paying for prepaid funerals and burial plots;
- Purchasing a new vehicle for the Community Spouse;

- Fixing up the house or even selling the old and purchasing a new house;
- Planning for the future of the Community Spouse.

You need to understand the nature of the prepaid funeral. This is typically an insurance policy you purchase through your family funeral home or religious organization. There are also banks that sell special CDs or accounts to be used for funerals. These are specialized policies and the Medicaid rules are usually quite stringent. It must be an irrevocable policy to be used only for the funeral and costs associated therewith. In Pennsylvania the amount of the policy varies from county to county. In Allegheny County (Pittsburgh) the current allowable amount is $15,550.00. This amount is to include the cost of the funeral, burial, casket, vault, wake, and other associated costs. It does not include the cost of the plot nor the stone or marker. We've had many clients tell us how glad they were that when the day of their loved one's passing came along, everything was completed and they did not have to worry about anything other than showing up for the viewing and funeral.

TIMING IS CRITICAL

You would not think that spending money would be a tricky, difficult area, but it is. Remember that we have this concept of a snapshot date. This is the date your spouse enters the facility. That is the date when your assets are measured, valued and totaled. The Community Spouse is permitted to keep one-half of these countable assets subject to a minimum and a maximum. I can best explain what makes this tricky by way of an example.

Jack's wife is suffering from Alzheimer's disease. He has done all he can to care for her at home. But the time has come to place her. He decides that before he does so, he best take care of some items. Jack goes out and buys a new car and gets a new roof put on his house. He spends $50,000 on these two items. Then he places his wife Cathy in a skilled nursing facility. He had $150,000 in countable assets, spent $50,000 and places her. He now has $100,000 at the time of applications. The caseworker informs Jack that he has $50,000 he may retain and must spend $48,000. Do you see the mistake he made? If Jack had waited until his wife was placed, he would have had $150,000. The case worker would have informed him that he had $75,000 to retain and would have spend-down of $73,000. At that point, Jack could buy his vehicle and new roof. He would now have only $23,000 remaining in spend-down. Jack made a $50,000 mistake by being pragmatic and logical. Medicaid is counter-intuitive. This is a very important concept to understand. Timing is critical.

THE COMMUNITY SPOUSE ANNUITY

Another important determination one must make early on is the answer to the question, What will be the income of the community spouse when the nursing home spouse passes? In a preceding section you learned about protecting the monthly income needs of the Community Spouse. You will learn that the Community Spouse is permitted to have income of a certain amount called a minimum monthly needs allowance (MMNA, currently $1,992.00 per month). If the Community Spouse's income is less than the MMNA, the Community Spouse may take income from the nursing home spouse. The Community Spouse keeps his/her own income and takes income from his/her nursing home spouse to make up the difference and reach his/her MMNA. What happens when the nursing home spouse dies? Will there be enough income for the Community Spouse who is now a single individual to continue to reach the MMNA? They've spent one-half or more of their life savings, so that is now gone.

You will learn more about MMNA and income the next section. Let's look at an example. Let's say that a Community Spouse receives $900 a month in income from Social Security and has a calculated MMNA of $2,100.00 under the Medicaid rules. In addition to her own $900, she collects $1,200 from her husband's income. Let's say that the nursing home spouse collects $1,400 from social security and $600 a month from a pension. The pension does not have a survivor benefit. The nursing home spouse passes away and the Community Spouse will have her income drop from $2,100 a month to $1,400. She will typically receive the greater of her or her spouse's social security income. Now she has spent one-half of her life savings and her income has been reduced by 33% to $1,400. Many an elder law attorney would have determined the viability of what we term a DRA annuity. DRA stands for the Deficit Reduction Act of 2005, a federal law. The DRA created new law with regard to how annuities are to be treated. The DRA creates a special, technical provision that allows a Community Spouse to purchase, with spend down funds, an immediate annuity that will essentially convert spend down assets into income. In this case the DRA compliant annuity could be purchased with spend down funds, enough to generate $700 a month. Thus, the Community Spouse would be able to receive her own $900 from her income, $700 from the annuity, and $500 from the nursing home spouse. When the nursing home spouse passes away, the Community Spouse will receive her husband's social security of $1,400 and $700 from that annuity.

This is a very technical area that I am describing with a broad brush. Just understand that this is an option that should be considered in many cases, especially where the Community Spouse will have a reduced income upon the passing of the nursing home spouse.

The DRA annuity usually has a provision that upon the passing of the Community Spouse, whatever proceeds remain unpaid by the insurance company that issued the annuity shall be paid over to the State Medicaid agency up to the value they paid out in Medicaid payments. There are other restrictions as well. Understand that this is an option you should consider and please see an elder law attorney about this option.

WHAT ABOUT GIVING THE MONEY AWAY INSTEAD OF SPENDING IT?

As you will see in the gifting section of this book, there is generally no gifting permitted. Currently there is a five year lookback where all gifts are aggregated and a penalty applied when the applicant is otherwise eligible. There are exceptions and sometimes it makes sense to make the gifts and pay through the penalty period. This is an especially useful strategy when the nursing home spouse has a high income and/or has long term care insurance paying a portion of the monthly bill. Ask your elder law attorney for continued advice in this area.

4. RULES REGARDING GIFTING

The five-year lookback. You've heard of it. Maybe you heard of the three-year lookback. Prior to February of 2006 it was a three-year lookback. Now it is five years and some people are pressing for a ten-year lookback. Those pressing for the ten-year lookback are selling or representing the long term care insurance industry. This is the biggest nightmare for everyone involved.

While I might refer to the transfers as gifts, the technical phrase is a transfer for less than fair market value. That is what causes the problem and that is the legal phrase. Many times I have been told that Dad did not give me the house, he sold it to me for a dollar. Thus, while not technically a gift, it is a transfer for less than fair market value. In other words, that is not going to work. What the "Fair Market Value" of an item might be is an art form and an area where we elder law attorneys are especially well trained.

APPLICATION OF THE GIFTING PENALTY

There is a penalty applied for all transfers for less than fair market value (gifting) during the five-year lookback. All such gifts are aggregated and totaled. When the person applying for Medicaid is "otherwise eligible," which essentially means has assets less than the amount allowed, a penalty of non payment for long term care costs is applied. They take this total amount and divide it by the average cost of nursing home care in your state. In Pennsylvania, the average is presently $8,766.39. Thus, if the gifting total was a little over $50,000, there would be a period of nonpayment of long term care Medicaid benefits for nearly six months. Who pays during that time period? That is a very good question. If the Medicaid applicant is single, he or she cannot have more than $2,000. How can he or she pay the nursing home bill? Let's just say, it's a problem.

People, particularly older people, enjoy bestowing gifts upon their loved ones. The trouble arises when they make gifts to their loved ones, and a few years later when they become ill, the whole matter comes out of nowhere and haunts them. As bad and draconian as it may sound, an elder law attorney can always help in this area as well. We've reduced or eliminated gifts by knowing how the law works and applying it to our clients benefit. How? There are a few exemptions, the most important of which is the law which essentially states that if the gift was made exclusively for purposes other than to obtain Medicaid eligibility, that gift is exempt. In our area, western Pennsylvania, the state caseworkers are taking the position that any transfer to a person that cannot be justified with a quid pro quo, a showing that the elderly person now applying got something of equal value in exchange, it is a gift and a penalty will be invoked. The representative of the applicant must then prove in an administrative legal proceeding that the transfer was not a gift but a transfer for value.

Done properly, by a professional, your family can retain a portion of your assets through gifting, even during the five-year lookback period. The key is to hire a qualified elder law attorney to assist you. Don't be concerned about the cost of the attorney. It is money you would otherwise spend on the nursing home. There are some circumstances where gifting is specifically allowed. Gifting is a very treacherous area and one that can have immense negative implications for both the resident / applicant as well as his or her family.

Even if gifting took place, innocently during the five-year lookback period, a good elder law attorney can minimize the damage or possibly even eliminate it entirely. The law provides exceptions if the gift was made exclusively for purposes other than to obtain Medicaid eligibility. The problem is that it is presumed that the gift was made for Medicaid purposes and can be a difficult burden to overcome. The proceeding is called a *fair hearing* in Pennsylvania. At a fair hearing we argue that the gift was made for purposes other than to obtain Medicaid. This can be a very strong argument if the applicant is in the nursing home due to the sudden onset of an illness such as a stroke. It can be a very difficult argument if the applicant was suffering from dementia and/or the gifts were made by way of a power of attorney.

In any event, there is usually some gifting that a good elder law attorney can do for you. Do not try to do it on your own. Seek help; it will cost you little in the long run. Remember, it is allowable spend down to hire an attorney.

Finally, understand what the five-year lookback really is. It is an audit period. The state is empowered to review the financial transactions of the applicant for the five years prior to applying for Medicaid. All transfers for less than fair market value (gifts) made during that five years are added together and the total amount is determined. Once the applicant is "otherwise eligible" (i.e. under $2,400 or $8,000 for a single person and under CSRA for a married couple), the penalty is applied. In Pennsylvania the average cost of a nursing home is $8,916.65. Thus, if the total gifting during the five-year lookback were $89,916, the Medicaid agency would not pay for ten months. Who pays? Good question. Someone will have to pay and nursing homes are very quick to hire collections attorneys to go after the people who were gifted the money. If that troubles you I understand. You'll have to speak with your congressman or senator about changing the law. This became the law in February of 2006 and is called the Deficit Reduction Act of 2005. It was not this way prior to 2006. Prior to 2006 the penalty began to run at the time the gift was made.

One last point: if there was a large gift made during the five-year lookback, it is critical that you do not make a major mistake by applying too early. This is best understood by way of example. Let's say a gift in the amount of $100,000 was made four and one-half years ago. If you apply now, the state should assess a penalty for one full year. You may ask yourself, "But there are only six months left in the lookback, why are they applying the penalty for one full year?" Understand that is how it works. If you were gifted $100,000 as shown in the example, you will need to pay for six more months to make it through the full five years. If you don't, you have big problems. Again, as I've stated over and over again, this book is intended to show you how dangerous the system is and why you cannot and should not attempt to try to do things on your own. You do not want the collections lawyers contacting or suing you. They can and they do just that.

GIFTING EXEMPTIONS
THE BUSINESS EXEMPTION
What if the person applying for Medicaid owns a business? Must that business be sold? Often times the answer is no. The business can be considered an exempt asset in many circumstances if someone is reliant upon it for their self-support.

THE DISABLED/BLIND CHILD EXEMPTION
There are exemptions from the gifting rules sometimes if the applicant has a child who is disabled or blind. Caution is warranted here as well. While there may be a gifting rule

exception, if that child is on SSI, he or she is not permitted to own more than $2,000.

THE CARETAKER CHILD EXEMPTION

There is also a special exemption from the gifting prohibitions related to the family home called the "care taker child exemption." This exemption permits a parent to gift their home to;

a) A child of his/hers;
b) Who has lived with the parent for 2 years or more;
c) Prior to entering a nursing home;
d) Who provided care such that the parent might have been unable to live in the home and in a nursing home much sooner had the child not lived with the parent.

These are the essential elements. Notice that it does not say grandchild, niece, nephew, or any such thing. It says child and it must be the child of the nursing home resident/applicant for Medicaid. The property must be the primary residence of the child and must have been for the two years prior to the parent entering the nursing home. This is also a law that gets interpreted differently in various counties and states. But it is important for you to know of its existence as a possible opportunity to preserve and protect your home from Estate Recovery.

The particular exemption gives rise to another area where a person, acting without the guidance of an experienced elder law attorney can get into trouble. Let's say, for example, that John lives with his mother and has for 10 years or more. As mom's age progresses, John convinces his mother to put the house into his name for fear that they might lose it if she has to go into a nursing home and apply for Medicaid. Mom complies. Two years later, mom goes into a nursing home and applies for Medicaid. The state agency that administers Medicaid benefits in their state assesses a penalty for the transfer of this house. Pointing to this particular law, John appeals. Does John win? Probably not. Why? Because one of the elements of the gift exemption implies that she must be in the nursing home before giving it to John. They were premature in making the transfer. There is a chance that the state caseworker would approve the transfer but there is a much better chance that it would get approved if John and his mother sought the advice and guidance of an experienced elder law attorney. From our experience as elder law attorneys, we have seen some counties allow these transfers if the child can prove it has been his or her home and primary residence for two years or more prior to the parent's admission. Other counties require a letter from the physician of the parent stating that the child provided extensive care that allowed the parent to remain at home. One county even went as far as to require the level of care provided to be skilled care of the sort provided at the nursing home. The law does not have that high a threshold but that is how they do it.

There are a few other exemptions that do not occur very often. For example, there is an exemption to give the home to the child of a Medicaid applicant under the age of 21. Most nursing home residents do not have children of that age. Still, it is an exemption on the books. There are a few more that are for disabled people and involve trusts. See you elder law attorney for more details.

CURING THE GIFT

Returning it can cure a gift and eliminate the penalty. If an elder gives a child $20,000 during the five year lookback and gets a penalty assessed because of that gift, the penalty can be eliminated if the child returns the gift. Of course the child would have to have the gift to return. If he or she does not, there is a real problem that, in some states, can subject the child to individual liability and a lawsuit.

A WORD ABOUT GIFTS AND TAXES

Have you heard that you are allowed to give away $10,000 or $12,000 or $13,000 or (now) $14,000. That is a tax law and NOT a Medicaid law. Frankly gifts and taxes rarely play any role in Medicaid cases. The tax free amount is a reporting amount. There is a $5,000,000.00 lifetime exemption. Gift taxes are best understood through an example. Let's say Glen, in 2014, gives his daughter and her husband $28,000. He also gives his son $14,000 and each of his ten grandchildren $14,000. This totals $182,000 in gifts. For gift tax purposes, he has not gone over the reporting limitation and his gift tax exemption has not changed. If Glen requires Medicaid for nursing home care within the next five years there is a huge problem. That gift of $182,000 will cause a massive penalty. In Pennsylvania, the penalty divisor of $8,766.39 will cause Glen to be ineligible for Medicaid for over 21 months. But for tax purposes, there are no concerns whatsoever. The gifting limit, $14,000 in 2014 is a gift tax limit, not a Medicaid limit.

Another example, let's say Glen gives $214,000 to his daughter. He has now exceeded the gift tax limit. He has exceeded the allowable limit by $200,000. How much does he pay in gift taxes? Nothing. However, his gift tax lifetime exemption will be reduced from $5,000,000 to $4,800,000. If he goes beyond $5,000,000 over his lifetime, he will pay taxes on any amount over $14,000 to an individual once the $5,000,000 has been exhausted. People with these asset levels are usually not too concerned about Medicaid and long term care costs. They are usually self insured. A person with $5,000,000 in Pennsylvania who entered a nursing home would have to be there for 49 years before running out of money and requiring Medicaid.

5. ESTATE RECOVERY

Another great pitfall in long term care is Estate Recovery. Estate Recovery is a federal law that mandates that each state have a program to seek reimbursement of the amount they paid out in Medicaid dollars from the estate of the deceased Medicaid recipient. For example, in Pennsylvania the state will not count your house if you are applying for Medicaid. Some children then believe that they can keep the house. They pay the taxes, utilities and insurance on the home to maintain it while their parent or loved one is alive and in the nursing home. They wrongfully believe that when the loved one passes, they will be able to keep the home. Upon the death of a person on Medicaid, the state has a priority position to get paid back for the value of Medicaid services provided. In Pennsylvania that recovery is currently limited to what goes through the Medicaid recipient's Will. There are usually only two assets, any term life insurance that the person had and failed to name a beneficiary or the named beneficiary is deceased, and the home.

People often talk about losing their home to the nursing home or to the state. It is Estate Recovery of which they are speaking. Many people are shocked to find that once their loved one passes away that the state has a large claim against the house. And the state must get paid back first. They will often state, "I was told that Mom could keep her house and still go on Medicaid." That is true. What was not understood was that the State would have a claim against the house, unless it was properly planned for. Everyone in Pennsylvania that applies for Medicaid for nursing home care is given a brochure on Estate Recovery. They are required to sign a form acknowledging that they received it. Most do not read it and many that do read it may not fully understand it.

States are not limited to recovering from the probate estate. Many states go after other assets such as trust assets, joint assets and other assets that pass by other than the Will. A few states, Florida for example, will not permit Estate Recovery to have a claim against a person's home because the home is protected from unsecured creditors by Florida's homestead exemption. Seek out the assistance of an elder law attorney in your state for assistance on this topic as well as all the others.

MISCELLANEOUS ISSUES
APPEALS
In Pennsylvania, the vast majority of cases get denied and then an appeal takes place. The state agency (called the County Assistance Office) has only so much time to approve an application, if they do not get it completed, they deny the application. Their grounds are typically that they did not receive all the information they requested. In order to keep the case alive, a simple appeal must be filed. This is usually no more than one sentence written on the back of the denial form stating the grounds for the appeal. During the pendency of the appeal, the case remains open and usually gets worked out.

This can be another dangerous area and one that has caught more than one lawyer by surprise. An example will prove useful in explaining the dangers. Bob and Mary apply for Medicaid for Mary's care. Bob has an annuity that used to be his IRA. Sometime in recent years Bob converted the IRA into an annuity and paid all of the income taxes due on it. He now owned an annuity valued at $20,000 that was not an IRA. This is a Pennsylvania case where IRAs owned by the Community Spouse (Bob in this example) are exempt. Bob's argument was that because it was an IRA before, it should continue to be viewed as an IRA. From the time Bob first sought eligibility until the appeal was heard was six months. The bill to the nursing home was $45,000. Bob argued his case and lost. Bob thought that because he lost, all he needed to do was pay the proceeds from that annuity to the nursing home and that would be the end of matters. Not so. Bob was instructed that their application was denied and that he would have to reapply. Reapply he thought? But this nursing home is owed $45,000 and I do not have it. Bob had a problem. An experienced elder law attorney would have helped Bob stay out of this danger.

BE AWARE OF YOUR STATE'S SPECIAL RULES

Everything described so far is only the tip of the iceberg. There are many other issues and laws that you may need to be aware of. But again, every state is different. For example, the Estate Recovery program requires the state to recoup funds from a deceased Medicaid recipient. Often times, that person had one large asset that he or she would have been able to hold onto after being found eligible for Medicaid, the family home. Estate Recovery is often the program whereby some family loses the home or its value to an Estate Recovery claim. At least one state that I know of does not enforce Estate Recovery claims if the property is the primary home and residence of the recipient. That state is Florida. Florida's constitution has a special section call the homestead exemption. In layman terms, the constitutional homestead exemption states that an unsecured creditor cannot seek to satisfy its claim by attaching the real estate of the debtor if that real estate is his or her home. Thus, while Florida's Medicaid agency may have an Estate Recovery claim, in most cases, it will not be able to satisfy that upon the death of the Medicaid recipient because of the homestead exemption. That property will pass to the spouse or children of the deceased Medicaid recipient.

DIFFERENCES IN APPLICATION OF THE CSRA

Earlier we discussed the CSRA, community spouse resource allowance. That has a federal minimum amount currently of $23,844. However New York has a minimum amount of $74,820. Some states exempt the IRA, 401K or other form of employer sponsored retirement plans from the resource allowance if that IRA or plan resource is owned by the Community Spouse. Pennsylvania and California are two of those states. Others do not. Most states count the IRA of the nursing home spouse as a countable asset.

These are but a few of the items that become issues in the Medicaid application process. Here's one more. What about the couple on their second marriage and they have a legitimate prenuptial agreement? In Pennsylvania that document is ignored. Pennsylvania follows the rule that if one spouse needs Medicaid, they must consider the assets of both of them regardless of the existence of a prenuptial agreement or not.

On-going Reporting Requirements and Redetermination

Medicaid eligibility is not a one-and-done type of deal. Eligibility is on-going. If the applicant's status changes, he or she leaves the nursing home, inherits money, or comes into additional income or assets by any form or amount, these all must be reported to the state agency that administers Medicaid typically within 10 days. In addition, every six months, or in some cases annually, a redetermination is made. The Medicaid recipient or his or her agent must complete a new set of documentation showing that circumstances had not changed and the individual remains fully eligible.

Failure to Disclose

Some people fail to appreciate the severity of the punishment of failing to disclose assets, income or other relevant items related to a Medicaid application or ongoing eligibility. The penalty is criminal fraud and theft of services. Most elder law attorneys will not be able to assist you with felony charges. Medicaid is not an issue to take lightly.

Conclusion

Medicaid is a great program. It can pay all of the long-term care costs of an elderly individual. That person has no medical bills. Medicaid covers whatever is not paid by other health insurance plans. Medicaid is also an extremely complicated, complex set of federal, state and local laws and rules. There is no room for mistakes in the Medicaid application process. Mistakes can cost you everything you own. Years ago I received a call from a lawyer who was helping a family friend appeal a Medicaid denial. When he ultimately lost his client's appeal, he thought all he had to do was make a payment in the amount of the discrepancy, $25,000. He was wrong. The Medicaid authority instructed him that because he lost, his client would have to apply all over again. "But … ", he exclaimed, "while we were waiting for this appeal to be decided, the family ran up a bill with the nursing home for over $70,000. They don't have $70,000." That's how it is with Medicaid. It's a great program, but the mistakes can cost you everything you own, and in some cases, more.

EXAMPLE - UNDERSTANDING CSRA
Cheryl and Ned Sample
Cheryl = Community Spouse
Ned = Nursing Home Spouse

On January 1, 2014 Ned is admitted to the Nursing Home. The nursing home costs $9,000 a month. On May 1 they have the following assets:

Checking Account (Joint)	$20,000	
Savings Account (Joint)	$50,000	
Certificate Deposit (3) (Joint)	$100,000	
IRA (Cheryl)	$ 50,000	
401k (Ned)	$100,000	
2012 Honda	$ 15,000	
Total Assets	$335,000	
Medicaid Exempt	$ 65,000	(Vehicle and IRA of Cheryl)
Total Countable	$270,000	
Retained by Cheryl	$119,220	
Retained by Ned	$ 2,400	
TOTAL RETAINED	$121,620	
TOTAL SPEND DOWN	$148,380	

This is a Pennsylvania-specific example. Cheryl's IRA is exempt, Ned's 401k is not exempt. Ned's 401k would be exempt if Ned were the Community Spouse. In Pennsylvania, most all employer sponsored retirement plans and IRAs are exempt assets provided they are owned by the Community Spouse.

Reverse the roles. Now Ned is the Community Spouse and Cheryl is the nursing home spouse. Now, the Medicaid exempt assets are Ned's 401k and the car. That totals $110,000. The total countable amount is $220,000. Ned, the Community Spouse keeps $110,000, Cheryl keeps $2,400, for a total of $112,400. Their total spenddown is now on $107,600.00. That's a difference of $44,000 in spenddown and a difference of $94,000 in the wealth of the couple. And the only difference is who was in the nursing home.

The Samples did not have a prior hospitalization and therefore have no Medicare coverage. On July 31, the Sample's have not spent any of their money. However, they are indebted to the nursing home at this time in the amount of $27,000 ($9,000 per month times 3 months). Their net countable spenddown is now $70,000. They visit an elder law attorney who explains everything to them. They then quickly spend $70,600 on prepaid funerals, the attorney fee and a new automobile. They pay the nursing home the $27,000 they owe and are now spent down. They are now eligible for Medicaid.

EXAMPLE - UNDERSTANDING MMNA

Cheryl and Ned are again our Community Spouse and Nursing Home Spouse respectively.

Ned's Monthly Income:
Social Security $1,504.90
Pension $500.00

Cheryl's Monthly Income:
Social Security $604.90.

Each has $104.90 deducted for their Part B Medicare premium. Ned also pays $200 a month for his health care premium. Thus Ned has available income $1,655.00. That is $2,004.90 minus $104.90 for Part B, minus $200 for his health insurance premium and minus $45 for his monthly personal needs allowance.

Cheryl pays a prorated $225 a month for real estate taxes and $30 a month for homeowners insurance. Her utilities are modest so she will be deemed to have monthly utility bills as determined by the State's standard utility allowance (currently $570.00). Her monthly shelter costs are $825 (225 + 30 + 570). The shelter standard is currently $598.00. Cheryl's monthly shelter expenses are in excess of the shelter standard by $227 (825 - 598). Her MMNA is then $2,219 which is $1,992 (the minimum) plus $227.00.

With Cheryl's income of $604.90, she has a shortfall of $1,557.10. The state will say that she is able to get a small interest amount from the assets she retains, but after that, she will receive the rest from her husband's income. If Cheryl is able to retain the maximum $119,220 in assets, the state will say that she can invest that and get a 1.5% return. They will essentially say that she can increase her income by $119,220 *1.5% / 12 per month. That is $149.00. Therefore, Cheryl will have her own income of $604.90, income from her assets of $149.00 and be able to make up the difference of $1,408.10 from her husband's income. Please note, that if Cheryl had an IRA, her required minimum distribution for that year would have to be determined, and they will also include that income for her on a monthly basis. So, if Cheryl had an IRA required minimum distribution for the year of $1,200.00, the State would attribute $100 per month of her income reducing the share her husband pays over to her by $100. So, in this example, Cheryl would be able to keep $1,308.10 of her husband's monthly income because of the IRA required minimum distribution attribution.

EXAMPLE - MISTAKES PEOPLE MAKE, SPENDING TOO EARLY

Nancy has Alzheimer's and her husband Clyde has been caring for her for years. It has gotten to the point where Clyde can no longer safely care for Nancy. Realizing that he will now have to find a nursing home for Nancy, Clyde decides he better take care of business. He and Nancy have $200,000 in their countable assets. Clyde goes out and spends $20,000 on prepaid funerals, $10,000 a piece. He also goes out and purchases a new vehicle for $30,000. He then places Nancy in a nursing home. Do you see the problem? Clyde made a $50,000 mistake. Clyde made these purchases before placing Nancy. He should have waited until she was placed. If he had waited, Clyde's resource allowance (CSRA) would be $100,000 and he would have $100,000 to spend (not counting Nancy's share). Clyde now spends the money on the funerals and vehicle and only has $50,000 remaining. Because Clyde did not wait, when Nancy went into the facility, on her snapshot date, they had $150,000. Clyde therefore can keep one-half, or $75,000 and has to spend $75,000. Clyde did what a think-ing, logical person would do in getting his and her affairs in order prior to placing Nancy. Medicaid, however, can often be counter-intuitive.

EXAMPLE - MISTAKES PEOPLE MAKE, SPENDING THE WRONG ASSET

Candy's husband Norbert is in a nursing home. They have bank accounts with $100,000 when Norbert goes into the nursing home in Pennsylvania. Candy also has a 401k from work valued at $200,000. For the next year, Candy pays for Norbert's care by taking withdrawals from her 401k. An accountant friend of hers told Candy that since Norbert is in a nursing home under a physician's prescription, the bills would be deductible from her income taxes. Therefore, Candy decides to pay for his care from her 401k. After a year, Candy applies for Medicaid and is denied because she has not spent down yet. They tell her the spend down is $50,000. She tells them she already spent $100,000. Do you see the mistake Candy made? Her 401(k) is exempt. Her spend down was from the $100,000 bank accounts and she has not spent any of that yet. All she needed to do was spend $50,000 from the bank accounts and her spend down would be complete.

EXAMPLE - MISTAKES PEOPLE MAKE, FAILING TO PLAN FOR THE FUTURE

Chelsea gets $800 a month in social security. Her husband Nate is in a nursing home. He gets $1,200 a month and $800 a month pension. However, when Nathan dies, Chelsea will not receive any of his pension. Chelsea rents and pays $800 a month in rent. Her MMNA is calculated to be $2,660.00.

Chelsea gets all of her income plus $1,860 of Nathan's income. They spend down their assets on Nathan's nursing home bill and apply for Medicaid. They receive Medicaid for a period of time until Nathan dies. Now, Chelsea learns that her income will only be the higher of her or Nathan's social security. She begins receiving $1,200 a month and that is the extent of her monthly income. Her rent is still $800 and she barely has enough income to pay for her other living expenses. She has a limited amount of assets because she has spent them down on the nursing home bill for Nathan. Chelsea has a large problem. She could have used a portion of her spend down to purchase a special annuity that would pay her a monthly income of $1,460 (Her MMNA of $2,660 minus her income when Nathan dies, $1,200).

EXAMPLE - MISTAKES PEOPLE MAKE, FAILING TO PLAN FOR THE CS DEATH

Connie has an IRA valued at $100,000. Her husband Neville and she have spent down and have a CSRA of $100,000. They also have a house valued at $200,000. They take no action to change their beneficiary designations or their Wills. Suddenly, right after Neville goes onto the Medicaid program, Connie dies. They have two children. The children learn for the first time that because they took no steps to change their estate plan, their father Neville is the owner of the home, the beneficiary of Connie's IRA and the beneficiary under Connie's old Will. Neville is now considered single and he is permitted to have no more than $2,000. The children are required to pay for his care and ultimately sell the house. If Neville lives for a few years, the entire life savings, IRA, and house may have to be liquidated to pay for his care. If they had done a little planning with an elder law attorney, they would have had to pay

143

over no more than one third (1/3) of the estate to Neville. The remaining two thirds would be paid to the children.

EXAMPLE - MISTAKES PEOPLE MAKE, DESTROYING THE IRREVOCABLE TRUST

The majority of elder law attorneys that do preplanning rely on an irrevocable trust that is called an Income Only Trust. That trust states the grantor, elderly person, will receive all of the income from the assets they give to the trust, but under no circumstances will the elderly person be able to have any access to any of the underlying principal (stock, mutual funds, etc that make up the trust itself).

Then, after that trust is formed and the assets placed in there, someone decides that the elderly person needs some more money and they write a check from the trust to the elderly person or to someone for the benefit of the elderly person. Remember the elderly person gets the income but not the underlying asset. If the elderly person is given anything that would be considered a payment from the trust of principal, the trust has been destroyed for its purpose of protecting assets for the five year lookback.

There is an old legal principle that states "course of performance in a contract overrules the written word." Thus, although the trust agreement says the elder has no access to the principal, if the trustee gives them principal, the course of performance trumps and the whole purpose of the trust's existence destroyed. Trusts can be the best form of estate planning with flexibility, security, and everything a person could want. They can also be tricky, dangerous instruments in the hands of a person without legal counsel.

EXAMPLE - MISTAKES PEOPLE MAKE, FAILING TO HIRE AN ELDER LAW ATTORNEY

Sonny lived with his mother for the past 10 years. As she began to age, she needed more and more assistance. Sonny moved in and took care of mom, catering to all of her needs until one day she got ill and went to the hospital. Following that, the hospital discharged her to a nursing home where she applied for Medicaid and spent the remainder of her years. When she died, Sonny was informed that the state had a claim for $135,000 dollars. Sonny informed them that the only asset she had was her home where he lived. The state officials told Sonny that he would have to sell the house and pay their claim. No one ever told Sonny about the child caregiver exception to the Medicaid gifting rules.

ELDER LAW ATTORNEYS

WHAT IS ELDER LAW

What is Elder Law? The Florida Bar describes Elder law as meaning legal issues involving health and personal care planning, including: advance directives; lifetime planning; family issues; fiduciary representation; capacity; guardianship; power of attorney; financial planning; public benefits and insurance; resident rights in long-term care facilities; housing opportunities and financing; employment and retirement matters; income, estate, and gift tax matters; estate planning; probate; nursing home claims; age or disability discrimination and grandparents' rights. The specialization encompasses all aspects of planning for aging, illness, and incapacity. Elder law clients are predominantly seniors, and the specialization requires a practitioner to be particularly sensitive to the legal issues impacting these clients.

Prior to the 1990s, elder law had a small, limited existence. Those lawyers who practiced in a field most closely associated with what we now call elder law were estates attorneys. Estates attorneys helped families manage the final affairs of a deceased loved one. They assisted families in the drafting of Wills, Powers of Attorney, Living Wills (also called Advance Directives) and Trusts.

Often times the focus of an estates attorney was on minimizing the amount the deceased individual's estate would pay in death taxes. There was a federal estate tax on the wealth of a deceased individual. Roughly speaking, this tax was nearly fifty percent (50%) of the amount of the estate (including life insurance) that was in excess of $600,000. Thus, the estate of an individual who passed away during that time period who had an estate valued at $1 million would have to pay approximately $200,000 in taxes. The problem was primarily for those individuals who owned a business when they passed away. Coming up with the necessary funds to pay the taxes became difficult. Many businesses had to be sold because they did not have the liquid funds available to pay the taxes. As a side note, that exemption is presently $5 million. Most people do not have to be concerned about it.

Their focus was and still is on taxes and the proper administration of the estate of a deceased individual. There are still numerous attorneys throughout the United States who still thrive in this area of law. While the exemption has skyrocketed, the necessity of the proper and orderly administration of one's estate is still, of course, required. Elder law includes these services as well. The difference, in my opinion, is that estates attorneys or estate planning attorneys, focus on either the very wealthy or business owners who want to maintain control over their business while at the same time provide for a change of ownership upon the passing of the owner without excessive, burdensome taxes.

Elder law attorneys handle estate matters as well. The distinction, or divergence, appears to have come about in the past 20 years because many people are now living longer. The focus is not so much on paying a portion of a deceased individual's accumulated wealth in taxes. Rather, in this day and age, modern medicine is keeping us all alive much longer. Many diseases and illnesses which terminated someone's life 20 years ago are now treated with a wide variety of ever increasing medicines and treatments. These people are living longer and while they are still living, their bodies are still aging and many of the things people used to be able to do, they cannot any longer.

You've seen it everywhere. Assisted Living Facilities, Personal Care Homes, Nursing Homes, Retirement Communities and the like are opening everywhere. People are living longer but they cannot continue to live independently as they had.

Managing the process and helping the individuals and their families with the wide range of choices they must make, without any prior experience, are now the job of the elder law attorney.

I've been practicing in this area for 20 years. Almost every client we have states at the outset "I've never had to do this before … I know nothing of this area." That's where an elder law attorney comes in. There is a whole lot more than just the payment of some taxes. A good elder law attorney, particularly one who practices life care planning (www.Lcplfa.org) is the most valuable resource you can find

Life Care Planning includes all of these areas but includes the more holistic needs of the family. Knowing what facilities are available, what programs are available, what benefits are available, where to go and how to pay for it all fall within the rubric of elder law for the life care planning attorney. For the life care planning attorney it's not just about the money. There's much more to it than the money. Being an experienced, skilled advocate and guide in finding the best place and getting the best care is the significant role of a life care-planning attorney.

THE BEST ADVICE

The best advice I can give you is to seek out the guidance and assistance of an elder law attorney, particularly a life care planning attorney. The mistakes you can make are numerous and extremely costly. While a mistake in estate planning under the guide of tradition estate planning might cost you more in taxes, mistakes in this field can cost you absolutely everything. In many cases, particularly those where an individual is in a nursing facility and will be applying for Medicaid, the cost of hiring an elder law attorney is nothing additional. Those cases involve what is termed "spend down" and the first and best spend down item is having a lawyer guide and assist you.

There are those who think and believe they are smart enough to handle it themselves. I completely understand that line of thinking. But there is one item that these individuals usually have not considered. They presume that the person with whom they are dealing understands the system and will apply the law as it reads. That is flawed thinking when it comes to Medicaid law. The area is so complex and complicated, many times the caseworker does not fully understand it himself. Many of them are new to the job or have been at it for a few years or less. On an almost daily basis when interacting with a state caseworker or nursing home employee, I will hear them state something that is completely wrong and contradicted by the law. A non attorney has no ammunition to challenge these people unless they have an elder law attorney. The defense "That's not what I was told" is not valid authority to submit a legal argument. One must be able to identify and point to valid statutory, regulatory or common law precedent to support their legal argument and buttress that with admissible factual evidence to support their position. The dangers one faces in the possibility of losing are much greater than the average individual anticipates.

How To Find An Elder Law Attorney

Elder law attorneys specialize in elder law. That is their practice area and they communicate it in no uncertain terms. Our firm's website is PittsburghElderLaw.com. Elder law is not a field where an attorney can dabble. Make sure you find one who does this type of work every day. There is far too much at risk as you will learn as you work your way through this book.

Ask around, check the Internet, talk with your financial advisor or accountant. Chances are they know the elder law attorneys in the area. Visit LCPLFA.org and see if you can find a life care planning law firm in your area.

You may see the designation CELA (certified elder law attorney). CELA is a designation that is provided by the National Elder Law Foundation. It requires an attorney to demonstrate their understanding of elder law and to take and pass a test. It is not Board certification and, because it is a national organization testing it, the CELA test is not state specific. In Pennsylvania where I practice attorneys do not have any sort of specialization title. Other states, such as Florida, have Board certification and frown upon any attorney claiming a certification or specialization unless that attorney is Board certified. Board certification is the recognition of specialization by the Supreme Court of that state. Both Board certification or the CELA designation can be helpful. These monikers will tell you that the individual has made something of a commitment to elder law. Ask around and find out who, in your area, practices elder law as their specialty.

Take a long look at Life Care Planning and the Life Care Planning Law Firms Association, www.LCPLPA.org. Life Care planning firms have the added benefit of employing elder care coordinators or elder care advocates to help you make all of the decisions for your loved one including their care. There are always questions and issues about care that come up where an elder care coordinator can assist. More importantly, if you've not found a facility or program for your loved one, then an LCPLFA firm in your area is invaluable. The role of the elder care coordinator in our firm is, among other matters, to help find and locate the right programs and facility for your loved one. Life Care Planning law firms go beyond the standard legal, financial advice provided by elder law firms.

Another great source for Pennsylvania, perhaps the best, is the Pennsylvania Association of Elder Law Attorneys (PAELA), www.PAELA.info. This a group of dedicated elder law practitioners.

If you are not sure in what direction to go, or where is the best place for your loved one considering all of their needs and abilities, a life care planning law firm can provide all of that. With life care planning law firms, the emphasis is not just on the money. It is also on getting the best care for your loved one.

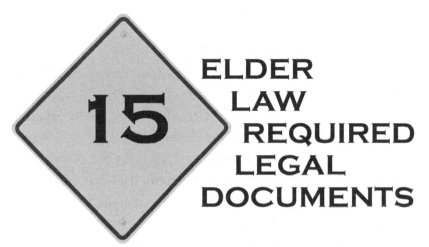

ELDER LAW REQUIRED LEGAL DOCUMENTS

This section will discuss basic documents everyone needs to have at a minimum for estate planning purposes: a Last Will and Testament, a Durable Financial Power of Attorney, and a Health Care Power of Attorney with a Living Will.

UNDERSTANDING THE NATURE OF ESTATES

Before we delve into basic legal documents, it is important that you understand how your assets will pass upon your demise. Not everything one has an ownership in passes through their Will. In fact, I would state to you that many items, more than 50%, do not pass through your Will.

What is in a person's sole name, with no beneficiary designation and no joint owners, will pass to the heirs through the Will. If an asset, such as an IRA or life insurance policy which has a beneficiary designation and the beneficiary designation was never filled out, or the person who was named in the beneficiary designation is already deceased, then that asset will be distributed according to the terms of the Will.

JOINTLY OWNED ASSETS

How many times have I heard someone describe to me a bank account that they own with another person. They'll say "It's an AND account!" or "It's an OR account. That really means very little except that it describes how many signatures are required for any check or other form of transaction. If a checking account is an AND account, that means that the signature of both account owners is required for any transaction. It that account is an OR account, that means that either one of the owners can sign checks.

When a person dies with a joint bank or investment account, in Pennsylvania if not in most states, the bank account becomes owned by the remaining joint owners. Thus if Tom and his son have a joint bank account and Tom passes away, the entire account is owned by his son and it is not subject the Will. If the account is owned by three people, the surviving two owners will inherit the account. If your state has a death tax, the tax will typically be based on the percentage amount owned by the deceased individual (50% subject to tax if two owners, 33.3% subject to tax if owned by three, etc.)

In many states, real estate is treated differently. Real estate can be owned as tenants in common or as joint tenants with rights of survivorship. If you ever saw the acronym JTWROS, that means joint tenants with rights of survivorship. Some states use the phrase *tenants by the entireties* for married couples. Tenants by the entireties means joint ownership between husband and wife. If real estate is owned by two people, and those two are not married, and there is no mention about joint ownership, in most states, upon the passing of one of the owners, that real estate will be owned 50% by the surviving owner and 50% by the estate of the deceased individual. This can have crucial consequences. First the surviving joint owner may find himself or herself owning real estate with another person whom they do not know or do not wish to cooperate with in the ownership of the property. Often times one wants to sell and the other does not. You can probably see how these issues can develop. Another problem develops when the deceased owner was on Medicaid and now has an Estate Recovery claim against that real estate since it is now part of the estate. (See Estate Recovery, Chapter 13).

There are other problems with joint ownership. Often a parent will add a child's name to an investment or bank account in order to allow that child to pay the bills of the parent when the parent passes. That can cause great inequities when the other children learn that one child received much more than the others. The joint account would pass solely to the surviving child owner on that account while all of the other assets are split equally.

Finally, when someone is on Medicaid, it is important that the account they are permitted to retain, whether it be $1,000, $2,000 or $15,000 (state dependent), be in joint names. Estate recovery may cause that account to be paid over to the state if it is in the Medicaid recipient's name alone. In many states, Pennsylvania in particular, Estate Recovery is limited to the probate estate (the Will). Since a joint account does not pass under the terms of a Will, Estate Recovery does not apply to that account (at least in Pennsylvania). How far the reach and scope of your state's estate recovery will be is an important matter for you to know. Ask your elder law attorney.

BENEFICIARY DESIGNATIONS

There are many assets that have beneficiary designations. These include individual retirement accounts (IRAs), 401ks, life insurance and annuities. Since each of these has a beneficiary designation, the asset will pass to those beneficiaries and the Will has no control over the distribution. Beneficiary Designations have become extremely popular. It is like a simplified Will. If there is no designation beneficiary, or the designated beneficiary has predeceased the owner, the beneficiary defaults to the Will. The problem with beneficiary designations is that you cannot place any restrictions or qualifications on the beneficiary's ownership. For example, as we will see in the Will section of this book, you can leave all of your assets to your spouse. But, you can place a restriction or qualification that provides that if you spouse should happen to be on Medicaid, or is in a nursing home for the long term, your spouse does not inherit the asset, rather it goes to your children or elsewhere.

POD / TOD / ITF ACCOUNTS

Payable On Death, Transfer On Death, In Trust For, these all have the same basic meaning and effect. These acronyms are associated with investment accounts, bank accounts and U.S. Savings Bonds. They are beneficiary designations for those

158

types of investments. If you see a certificate of deposit from a bank, and its ownership papers read "John W. Smith TOD Annie Smith" that means that John W. Smith is the full and complete owner of that account. When John dies, whatever is left in that account will be paid to Annie Smith. They work well for the most part and pass quickly to the beneficiary. The problem with them comes when one of them has to be liquidated. For example, let's say John Smith had three children, A, B and C. John has three $50,000 certificates of deposit, each of which has a POD beneficiary designation. Then John requires care in an assisted living facility. His checking account runs low and he needs to liquidate one of these CDs. Which does he choose? What if he has a Will that leaves everything equally to his children and these three CDs left to individuals? Then he has to liquidate one of these, or worse yet, his oldest child A, who has power of attorney for John has to liquidate one of these, which do they choose? What if A decides to liquidate the CD that has B as the beneficiary? A liquidates the CD and $30,000 of it is used for John's care before John dies. John has an estate comprised of the two $50,000 CDs and $20,000 in the checking account. A will get his $50,000 CD, C will get his $50,000 CD and the three of them will split the $20,000 in the checking after payment of the funeral and other expenses. You see the problem. You see why B might be a bit irate about what occurred. The efficiency of TOD/POD/ITF accounts is usually not enough to overcome the problems and inequities that occur far too often.

LAST WILL AND TESTAMENT

Any asset that has no beneficiary, and is owned individually by a deceased individual will pass through the Last Will and Testament. Often the Will is given a bad name because it is associated with probate. Probate is sometimes given a bad name by people selling investments that have beneficiary designation and part of their pitch is to claim avoiding probate as a benefit. Probate can be difficult in some states where the courts get involved from the outset. In other states, such as Pennsylvania, probate is an administrative process that is interfered with by no one until the person passes away.

The Will's greatest aspect is its ability to be flexible and adapt to the times. For example, in every Will we do for a married couple, there are three protective provisions. The Will usually provides that everything goes to my spouse but if my spouse has predeceased me, everything goes in equal shares to my children per stirpes. *Per stirpes* is a Latin phrase that essentially means that if a child has predeceased you, that child's share goes to that child's children. The first protective provision is for minor children. Minor children cannot inherit money. In Pennsylvania a minor is defined as anyone under the age of 18. If this provision does not exist, the attorney for the family would have to petition the court for a guardian of the estate to manage this money until the child turns 18 at which point the child would receive the money in full. Your Will should provide a protective provision that automatically establishes a trust for any minor so that Court appearance would be rendered unnecessary. Often people will increase the age to 21, 25 or even 30 years of age.

The second protective provision is for any heir who might be on supplemental security income, or on Medicaid already. This can be extremely powerful and important if any heir, who may happen to be on Medicaid, were to inherit from you. People on supplemental security income (SSI) are usually not permitted to have more than $2,000. In many states, such as Pennsylvania, if someone is on SSI, Medicaid is automatic. If they lose SSI, they lose Medicaid. They now have no income and no health insurance simply because they inherited money. While those things can be mended by the Courts, you are better off addressing it up front and putting the provision in your Will, just in case.

The third protective provision is for married couples. This provision states that if your spouse is in a nursing home or assisted living as the case may be, and will be there long term, his or her share of your Estate should be limited. We limit the share to one-third of the estate, which happens to be the amount of the elective share in Pennsylvania. See Chapter 13 which discusses Medicaid.

DYING WITHOUT A WILL

This has come up so many times I thought I would mention how your estate is handled and who gets what if you die without a Will. Again, this would only apply to non jointly owned assets and to those individually owned assets that do not have beneficiary designations. Your property will not go to the state. That is true for all 50 states. I don't know where that wives' tale ever started but it is not the case anywhere. Every state has a procedure called intestate (without a Will) succession. In Pennsylvania it works like this. If you are married and have children, all of whom are the children of your surviving spouse, the first $30,000 goes to your spouse and the balance gets divided one-half to your spouse and one-half to your children. If you are married and have children, some of whom are not the children of your spouse, your spouse gets fifty percent and your children split the other fifty percent. If you are not married, everything gets split between your children. If you have no children, it goes to your parents. If your parents are deceased, to your brothers and sisters. If they are deceased, to your nieces and nephews. If there are none of any of those, your closest relatives will have to be determined and they get everything. If no relatives can be found, the property goes to the unclaimed property division of the state in which you resided at death.

Durable Financial Power Of Attorney

What would you think is the most important estate planning document one must have? The answer is the durable financial Power of Attorney (POA) in most cases. The POA will empower your chosen agent to pay your bills, sign contracts for you and otherwise manage your affairs. Unless the POA states otherwise, a POA does not empower your agent to steal from you. POAs are usually revocable and the agent is held to a legal standard, called a fiduciary standard, to always act in the best interests of the person who gave the agent his or her authority. That person is called the principal.

We often get calls from people who need to have a power of attorney done immediately. The story usually begins with a statement that a loved one is in the hospital and the hospital needs to speak with the person who has the power of attorney, the agent. They explain that they do not have one and call our office looking for us to draft a power of attorney. There are many problems at this point. Often the person for whom POA is sought is unable to sign his or her name. Another is that the person can sign but would not understand the nature of what they are signing. In both of these circumstances, a POA cannot be used. If the person cannot sign or would not understand what it is they are signing, the POA will not work. At this point the family has to obtain the services of a lawyer and petition a court to appoint a guardian (in some states called a conservator) for the person. Guardians can be of the person or the estate. A guardian of the person makes the health care and medical decisions for someone; a guardian of the estate makes financial and asset decision for the person. The person over whom guardianship is sought is also known as the ward. Guardianship proceedings can be expensive and have a number of legal requirements that must be followed. It can be a difficult experience.

You can avoid ever having a guardianship by merely having an attorney draft and you sign a power of attorney. You choose who will act in your best interests, not the court. A Court can appoint anyone it sees fit to act as a guardian for someone. It does not have to be a family member.

There is one last point for you to understand. If someone gives you power of attorney, when that person dies, your authority also dies and you may no longer use the power of attorney. Over the years there have been many times when a person thought they were a joint owner on a bank account only to learn later that their name was on that account as power of attorney (you may also see the phrase attorney in fact, it means the same thing). Thus, if there is a bank account with two names on it and the second is on there as power of attorney, when the first person dies, the bank account does not automatically go to the power of attorney but will be distributed to the heirs of the Will.

HEALTH CARE POWER OF ATTORNEY - LIVING WILL

A Living Will states what measures you want to be taken to be kept alive if two or more doctors certify that you are dying. Usually people want no measures taken other than comfort and relief from pain. A few people want any and all actions taken to keep them alive. It's a matter of personal preference. It used to be all that one needed for health care decision making was a Living Will. However, today with the advent of HIPAA (Health Insurance Portability and Accountability Act), also known as the privacy rule, Health Care Powers of Attorney became prevalent. A HIPAA compliant power of attorney will authorize health care providers to discuss your care and share your records with the person whom you appoint as your health care power of attorney.

Also, because we are now living longer and often times in a long term care facility, it has become necessary to appoint another as the one to make all of your health care decisions if you are unable to make them on your own. That person can decide what facility you will go to and the extent of the care you will receive. There are also decisions regarding a DNR (Do Not Resuscitate) order. A DNR is a hospital signed document that states that if you go into cardiac arrest, they are to take no measures to keep you alive including CPR. CPR often involves the breaking of one's rib cage to get to the heart to keep it beating. That type of traumatic care can be devastating and painful to frail, elderly people. Make sure you have a HIPAA compliant power of attorney signed as well as a living will. Give a copy of each to your primary care physician and to any long term care facility where you might reside.

OPTIONAL DOCUMENTS
TRUSTS, TESTAMENTARY VS. LIVING & REVOCABLE VS. IRREVOCABLE

The concept of a trust is foreign to most non-lawyers. Trusts developed under the old English legal system. At its root, a trust is a contract with three parties, the person who sets up the trust and places money or assets into it (called the Grantor or Settlor), the person whose job it is to manage the assets and have control of them (called the trustee) and the person who is to benefit from the trust (called the beneficiary). Trusts were established hundreds of years ago when a young man from England signed up to join a ship which was to sail to a foreign land to obtain goods such as spices, gold, and the like. While he was gone, he contracted with another man in the community to manage his affairs and care for his family. He chose someone he 'trusted'. These agreements were known by and enforced within the community. The trustee could do whatever he wished with the trust assets. He was bound by the contract he signed to manage the assets for the benefit of the person(s) listed as beneficiaries. For many years, banks have had trust departments to manage trust assets for the very wealthy.

A revocable living trust has been popular in this country for the past 40 years or so. They have been used by people to manage their own assets but have a plan in place to manage their assets in the event of their disability and upon their death. Typically, with a revocable living trust, the grantor, trustee and beneficiary are the same person. However, in the event of the disability of the grantor there would now be a new trustee and the disabled grantor would remain as beneficiary. Upon the passing of the grantor, a new trustee steps in and either distributes the trust assets or continues to hold the trust assets and manage them for a new beneficiary as the trust agreement dictates.

A trust can be created in a person's Last Will and Testament (called a Testamentary Trust) or while alive (called a Living Trust). A trust can also be revocable or irrevocable. Most living trusts today are revocable and thus completely changeable. You can add assets to the trust, remove assets from the trust, change the trust terms or completely dissolve the trust. Most people with revocable living trusts do not have to file a special income tax return (called a fiduciary return, Form 1041). Typically though, a revocable living trust uses the social security number of the grantor who is also the trustee and beneficiary. Usually, the three parties to a revocable living trust are all the same person. Revocable living trusts are of little or no benefit when it comes to long term care planning and asset protection for long term care costs. Because the trust is revocable and because the beneficiary can change or dissolve the trust and get his or her hands on the trust assets, they are available assets for most long term care programs such as Medicaid.

An irrevocable living trust is different. Many skilled and adept elder law attorneys use irrevocable living trusts to help family's shelter assets in the event of long term care costs. Irrevocable living trusts have always been subject to a five year look-back. It would be completely foolish for anyone to attempt to create and fund an irrevocable living trust on their own, without the assistance and ongoing guidance of a skilled elder law attorney. You must be very careful when utilizing one of these trusts. Case in point. As I stated, a trust is a contract. One of the long-held principles of contract law is that course of performance is a better indicator of the terms of the contract than the written word itself. Thus, if an irrevocable living trust states that under no circumstances may the grantor (the person who funded the trust) have access to the underlying assets, but the trustee goes ahead and writes checks to the grantor or for his or her care anyway, you have a situation where the trust may be declared invalid for purposes of sheltering assets for Medicaid or some other long term care program. Use an elder law attorney for this as well as any other long term care planning. The stakes are too high. See Optional Documents for more information about Irrevocable Living Trusts for asset protection.

Special Needs Trust

If you have a disabled child or heir, and that person is receiving supplemental security income (SSI) and/or Medicaid, that person is limited to the amount of assets they are permitted to have and receive SSI. For most people on SSI, Medicaid is automatic. If you lose SSI, you lose Medicaid. If you come into too much money, you lose SSI and Medicaid and now have no health insurance. It is important to understand the type of coverage anyone has who is disabled and may inherit from you. If that is the case, you may want to speak with your elder law attorney about the drafting of a Special Needs Trust. This type of trust will allow you to leave money to the disabled heir in a trust that will not affect his or her SSI but will still have money available for him or her through the Trust.

Life Estate Deed

A life estate deed also is derived from old English law. A life estate deed is a deed. It essentially states that upon my death, ownership of this property shall vest in another person. It is not joint ownership. With joint ownership, more than one person owns the property. With a life estate deed the property is owned and controlled by the person who owns the life estate. That person can do whatever they wish with the property except for one thing. They cannot sell the property to another. They own it, control it, and are responsible for it for the remainder of their life. But, when they die, ownership vests automatically in the other person (called the remainderman in legal terms). The property can be sold to another if the remainderman agrees to the sale.

People will use a life estate deed to protect their property from being subject to estate recovery in the event they end up in a nursing home on Medicaid. As with everything else, a life estate deed can be tricky. If you sign a new deed to your property and it is a life estate deed, you have made a gift. That gift is subject to the five year look-back like anything else that would be considered a gift. Also, if the person who has the life estate sells the property, when all parties agree to it, they are legally entitled to a percentage of the sale proceeds based upon tables established by the Social Security Administration. Therefore, if someone establishes a life estate deed, and eventually ends up in a nursing home, that property cannot be sold. If it is sold, a portion of the proceeds must be given to the grantor and that may cause the grantor to lose Medicaid. We've created an app on the iTunes store to help you calculate life estate values. It's called the Estate Planners Assistant. It's also on Google Play. Or, if you wish, you can google life estate tables and do your own calculations once you locate the tables.

JOINT OWNERSHIP DEEDS

A long time plan for people wishing to protect their home is to put their children's name on the deed. Putting anyone's name on your deed means that they have an ownership interest in the home. If you put your home entirely into your children's name(s), you have given them your home. There are clear and obvious dangers in doing so. There are also dangers that are not so clear, for you and for your children. I once had a case where a family put their home into their sons' names. One son died in a car accident two years later. A year after that, the father went into a nursing home and had to apply for Medicaid. The house could be returned to the father and that would have cleared up the Medicaid gifting problem. However in this case the son's estate was being sued by others who were injured in the accident he caused. In addition, the mother/wife was still alive and living in the home. The parties suing the son were against anyone trying to change ownership in the home. It was a real mess. This can happen to anyone. In addition, if you give your home to your children, they will have to pay a capital gains tax when they sell it. This can be 15% - 20% of the gain. The parents would not have this problem because for the most part your home is exempt from capital gains taxes. However, because the children do not live in the home it is not their home but an investment property essentially. Therefore, when they sell the property they will have to pay what might be a hefty capital gains tax.

THE HOME, CAPITAL GAINS, AND STEP UP IN BASIS

Briefly stated, capital gains taxes are calculated by taking the sales price and subtracting the parents' basis (what they paid for it and put into it). That is called the gain. Multiply the gain by the capital gains rate of 15% - 20% and that is the amount they must pay in capital gains taxes. If they had inherited the house, the basis becomes the fair market value at date of death. If they sell the house at fair market value at the time of death, there are no capital gains taxes. On the other hand, the house may be subject to being lost to long term care costs which is more than a percentage paid in taxes, it is everything! There can be an answer to this dilemma. A deed with a life estate means that the person does not acquire full ownership until the grantor dies. Thus there is a step up in basis for the person who inherits through a life estate deed. In addition, certain irrevocable trusts can also be used to protect the assets from long term care costs as well as capital gains taxation. See your elder law attorney for assistance with this matter.

ANNUITIES

A very unique animal is the annuity. Annuities come in various flavors and types. They may be variable, index driven or fixed. Some people use them as an alternative to certificates of deposit. Annuities were designed to be retirement income for people much like an individual retirement account. You put money into the annuity and they grow tax deferred. When you reach a certain age you must start taking the money out of the annuity and paying the taxes on the part that is income. In addition, an annuity can be annuitized. By annuitizing an annuity, you are turning that lump sum asset, its value, into a stream of income. If you have an annuity you can annuitize it over a period of years, or your life. There are many different terms based upon the annuity contract. Annuities are issued by life insurance companies. The concept of providing a steam of income instead of a lump sum can be very attractive to people. Elder law attorneys make use of annuities in many ways. We will often take spend down money for a married couple and purchase an annuity that will guarantee the Community Spouse (the one not in the nursing home) a stream of income for the remainder of his or her life. There are catches to this annuity. The biggest catch is that upon the death of the Community Spouse, whatever amount remains in that annuity must be paid to the State Medicaid agency. Still, the money is spend-down and having a guaranteed stream of income to the community spouse is very valuable.

Annuities can also be a great way to protect someone who is not able to manage money. Instead of leaving a lump sum of cash to a person, you can leave them an annuity payable to a term certain. You have given them a steam of income instead of a lump sum of money. That can be a very valuable estate planning tool.

Finally there are a few long term care strategies used by elder law attorneys that help protect assets. These strategies are advanced and beyond the scope of this book. See an elder law attorney in your area for more information.

If you have questions, please feel free to email me at carl@ pittsburghelderlaw.com.

Thank you. I hope you enjoyed this book and I hope it made you understand the long term care maze a little better and safer for you.

Made in the USA
Columbia, SC
24 June 2018